Three-Fold Path

Way to True Awareness

A Journey Within to
Peace, Joy & Harmony

Teachings by Sri Ashish

ISBN

Hardcase: 979-8-9932716-0-6

Paperback: 979-8-9932716-1-3

Published By:

An Imprint of NDP Foundation Inc.
www.ndpfoundation.com

This Book is dedicated to
all Masters of Self-Realization

The Eternal Truth

How profound—the Self shines clear,
Untouched by illusion, ever near.
No stain can mark its boundless light,
It stands alone, serene and bright.

How eternal—the Self does stay,
Beyond all birth and death's decay.
It neither comes, nor does it flee,
It simply is, eternally free.

How complete—no lack, no part,
It holds the whole within its heart.
Nothing missing, nothing more,
Perfect peace at its core.

How still—it does not move or bend,
Yet all arises, begins, and ends.
The play unfolds within its grace,
While it remains in silent space.

How limitless—without a seam,
It births the world and every dream.
Ten billion forms, yet always one,
Effortless, like rays from the sun.

I offer thanks to the **Divine Source** within us all—the formless, infinite Self that animates every experience and expression. May these teachings serve as a reminder of the undisturbed peace, joy, and freedom that are your birthright, always present within you.

Sri Ashish (2025)

"Beyond 'I AM'– Nothing is
Within 'I AM'– Everything is"

Table of Contents

About NDP Foundation

NDP (Non-Duality Perspective) Foundation is dedicated to the awakening and realization of the timeless Truth — that at the heart of all existence is one undivided, silent, and still Presence. Founded on the insights and lived experience of Sri Ashish, the foundation serves as a guiding light for those on the path of self-discovery and inner transformation. Rooted in the essence of Non-duality (Advaita) and expressed through the integrated wisdom of the Three-Fold Path - Right Understanding, Right Practice, and Right Experience, the Foundation's work is centered on helping individuals realize their true nature as Pure Awareness. The mission of NDP Foundation is not to promote a new belief system, but to offer tools, guidance, and reflective inquiry that bring seekers into direct contact with their innermost being.

Through publications, retreats, community learning, and Awareness-Based Living programs, the Foundation works to *preserve, propagate, and perpetuate* the essence of these teachings for generations to come.

NDP Foundation publishes all printed books under these three imprints - Three-Fold Path Publications; Presence Publications; and I AM Publications.

Whether you are just beginning your inward journey or deepening your practice, NDP Foundation offers a space where clarity unfolds, stillness deepens, and the Self is gently remembered.

About Sri Ashish

Sri Ashish is a contemporary teacher of Advaita Bhakti—non-dual devotion, which honors the Oneness of everything and the Oneness in everything. Known for his clarity, humility, and transformative insight, Sri Ashish's teachings emerge not from scholarship alone but from profound personal experience. His words do not come from borrowed knowledge but from lived realization, forged through deep inquiry and tested by life's most intense trials.

Born in Kolkata, India, Sri Ashish's early life followed the arc of conventional success. Educated in electrical engineering in the United States, he returned to India to lead a family business, later becoming a successful entrepreneur in sectors like information technology, telecom, and renewable energy. Yet beneath the surface of worldly achievement, a growing inner unrest stirred. Between 2008 and 2016, his life was shaken by a series of profound personal losses. These events dismantled the foundations of his identity and ignited a search for meaning beyond the material world. What began as a cry for help in the depths of despair evolved into a transformative spiritual journey. Guided by a spontaneous inner calling and drawn to the teachings of Paramhansa Yogananda and Sri Ramana Maharshi, he immersed himself in meditation, self-inquiry, and the ancient science of yoga. What followed was a gradual but irreversible shift—a direct realization of the Self beyond all roles, concepts, and suffering.

Sri Ashish does not identify as a guru, swami, or master. "These are labels," he says, "that create expectations and illusions." Rather, he sees himself simply as a householder and seeker who, through suffering and perseverance, stumbled into a doorway of Truth.

From this realization emerged the Three-Fold Path—a simple yet profound synthesis of Right Understanding, Right Practice, and Right Experience that invites each person to return to their true nature as Pure Awareness.

He now shares this path through writings, talks, and the NDP (Non-Duality Perspective) Foundation, which serves as a platform to make these teachings available to all—regardless of background, belief, or readiness. His presence is open, warm, and inclusive. In his words, "The door is open to all—whether you're curious, searching, or even skeptical. There is no hierarchy here, only the invitation to remember who you truly are."

Through the Three-Fold Path, Sri Ashish gently guides seekers back to the stillness that is their origin. He offers not a belief system but a mirror—pointing directly to the unchanging awareness that lives silently behind every experience. In that silence, suffering ends. In that stillness, Truth shines. In that awareness, we are whole.

Prologue: The Journey Home

Life, in all its complexity, rests upon a simple truth: ***"I AM."*** This awareness, silent yet ever-present, is the essence of who you are. It is not something to achieve or acquire but something to uncover, like the sunlight hidden behind clouds.

To journey through life is to walk the path of discovery. Some seek wealth, others seek purpose, and many search for happiness in distant lands. Yet, the greatest journey is not outward, but inward.

A young seeker once set out to find the truth of existence. He traveled far and wide, seeking wisdom in sacred texts, in the words of sages, and in the depths of solitude. He climbed the highest peaks, crossed vast deserts, and meditated under ancient trees, hoping to find what his soul longed for.

One day, weary from his search, he sat beneath a quiet sky and listened—to the wind, the rustling leaves, the steady rhythm of his own breath. And in that stillness, truth revealed itself: ***He was never separate from it.***

The seeker's path is not about becoming more but about **unveiling what has always been within.**

It is a path walked with:

- **Openness**—for wisdom arises where the mind is free.
- **Stillness**—for truth emerges when noise fades.
- **Courage**—for awakening requires bravery to let go.

The Three-Fold Path is a journey to rediscover this truth. It offers clarity through Right Understanding, stability through Right Practice, and fulfillment through Right Experience.

Inspired by my own journey, this book serves as both a roadmap and a companion for those ready to explore the depths of their being.

This is not a journey of becoming something new; it is a return to what you have always been.

Reality and the Illusion

The Process of Creation and Self-Realization

The Dance of Reality and the Illusion

From the silent depths where no time flows,
Reality, eternal, endlessly glows.
Formless, nameless, vast, and free,
The essence of all that comes to be.

Yet, in stillness, a whisper stirs,
A spark within the silence occurs.
"I AM" awakens, a luminous flame,
The first of knowing, the birth of name.

From "I AM," the dream unfurls,
A tapestry of infinite worlds.
Ego rises, a fleeting spark,
Casting shadows in the cosmic dark.

The mind takes hold, weaving its tale,
Of joys and fears that rise and fail.
Through body and form, the story plays,
A fleeting dance of nights and days.

But beneath the waves of thought and strife,
Reality whispers: ***You are Life****.*
Not the mind, nor body, nor fleeting name,
But the silent witness, ever the same.

The drop and ocean, wave and sea,
The truth unveiled: there's only Me.
No lines to mark, no bounds to find,
Reality, formless, leaves all behind.

To awaken is not to seek or gain,
But to dissolve the ego's chain.
A journey back, a path unmade,
Through layers of illusion, the truth displayed.

Detach from form, from ego's veil,
Let stillness guide, let silence prevail.
Rest in the "I AM," the anchor, the key,
And know the Self as boundless and free.

Beyond even "I AM," the Absolute calls,
A presence where no shadow falls.
Not one, not two, not here, not there,
Just infinite being, pure, aware.

So dance with the dream, but know it's light,
A play of forms in endless night.
For Reality waits, serene and whole,
The eternal essence, the source, the soul.

Reality and the Illusion: The Process of Creation and Self-Realization

Creation and Self-realization are two ends of a continuum in which the essence of existence unfolds and returns to its source. Creation is the imagination and projection of Consciousness appearing on Reality, a timeless and formless essence, in a world of form and appearance. Self-realization is the journey back — an awakening to the unchanging truth that has always existed within. This segment explores the process of creation from Reality to Consciousness to the phenomenal world and outlines the path to Self-realization as described in the Three-Fold Path.

What is Reality? This question has been asked by philosophers, scientists, and seekers of truth across time. The answer, as simple as it is profound, lies not in the realm of thinking but in direct awareness.

Reality is not something that can be described or defined; it transcends conventional descriptions and definitions. It embodies pure awareness and existence. It is devoid of attributes, desires, time, or space. Reality is eternal, unchanging, and pervades all equally, serving as the foundation of existence itself. It exists independently of memory, perception, or any sense of objectivity, preceding all knowledge. It is formless, nameless, and embodies the essence of Self. It is existence itself, untouched by thoughts, emotions, or the appearances of creation.

The teachings of the Three-Fold Path are grounded in this understanding, inspired by ancient wisdom and illuminated by direct inquiry. This book invites you to explore the layers of existence, from the ego and mind to the awareness of **"I AM,"**

Reality and the Appearance of Creation

Reality → Consciousness → Creation (Ego/Mind/Body/World)

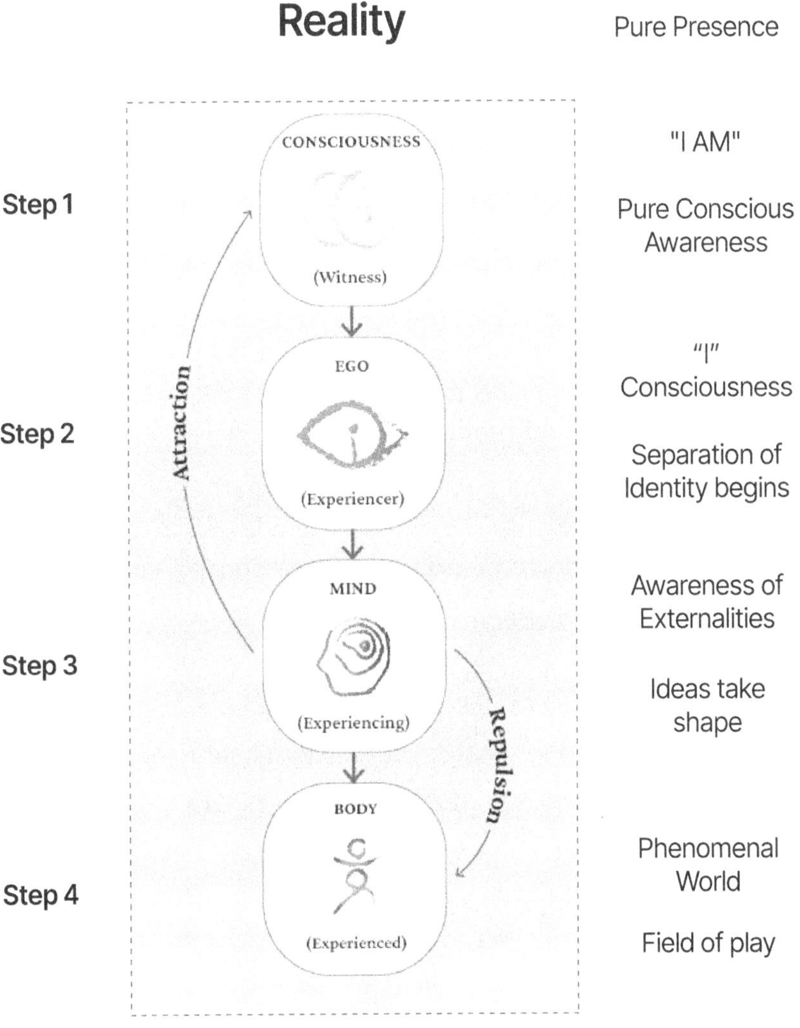

Note: The dotted box encompasses the ***appearance*** *of the illusion on* ***Reality*** *(blank canvas).*

Diagram 1: Reality and the Appearance of Creation

and ultimately to transcend even this awareness to rest in the Absolute (Reality).

Reality (*Parabrahman* , Absolute): The Source of All

At the heart of existence lies Reality (Presence, Existence, or Being), the eternal Spirit or Self which is the singular, indivisible, and unchanging essence. In ancient scriptures this essence is referred to as *"Sat" or "Truth,"* the underlying presence from which all existence appears to emanate. Reality is formless, nameless, timeless, and spaceless, existing beyond attributes and qualities. It is Pure Presence — a state of AM-ness. Reality does not act, think, or create in the way we commonly understand; it simply *is*.

However, human comprehension of this eternal essence is clouded by illusions of the ego and mind, which confines awareness to the material realm and its sensory objects.

Characteristics of Reality:

- *Eternal, luminous, profound, unconditioned, and self-effulgent.*
- *Devoid of subject-object relationships or duality.*
- *Existence itself, pervading everything equally.*
- *Silent, still, and thought-free.*

In spiritual terms, Reality is often described as the blank canvas or movie screen upon which the play of creation unfolds. The canvas or the screen remains untainted, providing the foundation for all appearances but does not create or become altered by them.

Appearance: From Reality to the World

The process of creation begins with the spontaneous appearance of "I" on the "AM" - " **I AM** " – Pure Conscious Awareness or Consciousness on Reality which imagines and activates the appearance of creation as ego/mind/body and the phenomenal world. This appearance occurs in distinct stages, each adding illusive layers of individuality and separation to the unified essence.

Stages of Creation as Appearance:

Reality to Consciousness:

Consciousness appears spontaneously of its own volition on Reality or Pure Presence (Existence or Being) creating an appearance of Pure Conscious Awareness. This is where the first sense of awareness or the development of recognition occurs. This is often described as the "I AM" state or *Sat-Chit-Ananda (Being-Awareness-Bliss or Existence-Consciousness-Bliss)* — the universal witness, the silent observer, a subtle shift from pure being into the realm of recognition. It serves as the dreamer of the universal dream, initiating the imagination and appearance of creation. It pervades everything and is the creator, sustainer and destroyer of all illusion.

In Reality (*Self or Sat*) resides the origins of all knowledge, love, power, and joy. These divine qualities manifest in two forms:

1. **Cosmic Consciousness (Chit):** The essence of awareness that illuminates existence – the divine light (*Kuthastha Chaitanya*).
2. **Force (*Shakti, Nature, Ananda*):** The creative power that initiates movement and change. Originator of the Cosmic Deluder or Illusion *(Maya)*.

Consciousness to Creation – Ego/Mind/Body/World:

Development of the idea of Ego:

Consciousness cannot remain idle for long, so it begins to differentiate, giving rise to the idea of a separate individual identity (Ego).

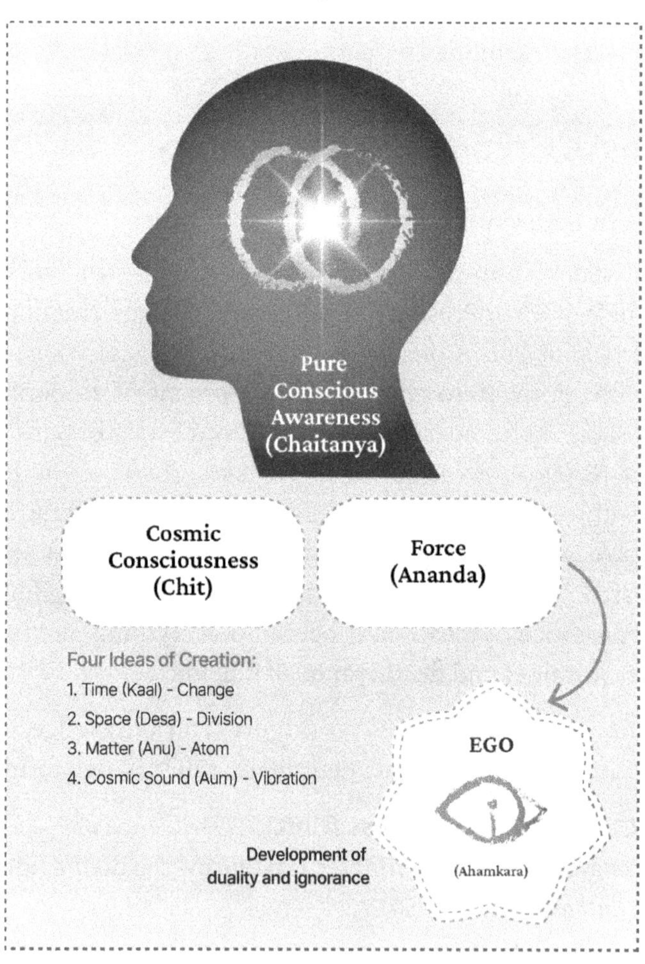

Note: The dotted box encompasses the **appearance** of the illusion on **Reality** (blank canvas)

Diagram 2: Development of the idea of Ego

The Ego represents the idea of individuality, the sense of "I AM this or that" or "I-consciousness" as separate from the whole - the beginning of experiencer-experiencing-experienced stage. This stage is characterized by the development of duality and ignorance (forgetfulness of the true Self). The ego originates by the reflection of the divine light through the four main ideas or concepts of creation - space, time, matter and vibration (cosmic sound).

This is where the illusion of separation takes hold, leading to the perception of a fragmented reality.

Ego pervades all thoughts – Ego to Mind:

The ego's sense of individuality operates through the mind. The mind is a complex structure, encompassing thoughts, emotions, memories, and impressions. It operates through five layers (sheaths) — physical, energetic, mental, intellectual, and blissful. These layers give rise to perceptions of identity and personality.

Pure Conscious Awareness (" I AM") emanates divine love and attraction, guiding creation toward spiritual unity. The same awareness when reflected through the constructs of the ego and the mind generates repulsion from spiritual unity towards separation and diversity. This is where the tug of war between the dual-faceted state of the mind occurs through:

- **Intellect (*Buddhi, Attraction*):** Oriented toward truth and spirituality.
- **Blind Mind (*Manas, Repulsion*):** Ego-driven and focused on sensory experience.

Appearance of Body – Mind to Body

The mind's interaction with the five elements (earth, water, fire, air, and ether) through its fifteen instruments (five senses, five of locomotion (hands, feet, mouth,

Reality (Sat)

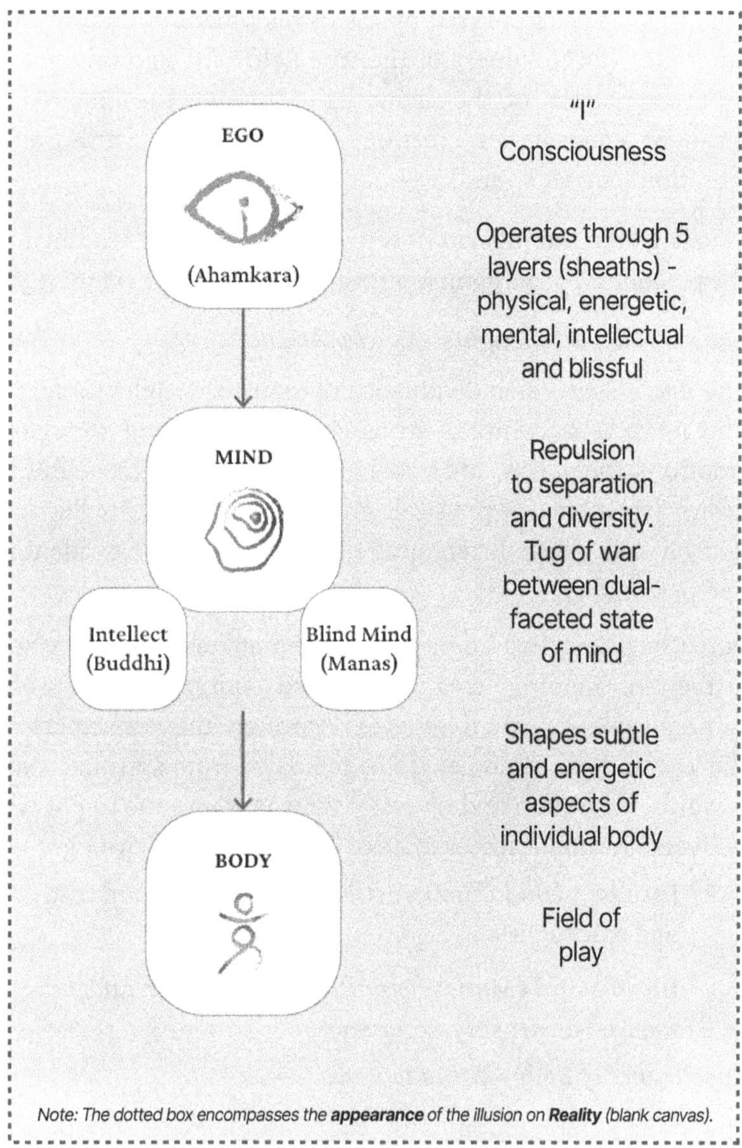

EGO
(Ahamkara)
MIND
Intellect (Buddhi)
Blind Mind (Manas)
BODY
"I"
Consciousness
Operates through 5 layers (sheaths) - physical, energetic, mental, intellectual and blissful
Repulsion to separation and diversity. Tug of war between dual-faceted state of mind
Shapes subtle and energetic aspects of individual body
Field of play
Note: The dotted box encompasses the **appearance** of the illusion on **Reality** (blank canvas).

Diagram 3: Play of the Mind

procreation and excretion), and five breathes or *pranas* controlling the involuntary functions of crystallization, assimilation, metabolism, circulation, and elimination), shapes the subtle and energetic aspects of the individual idea crystallizing as the physical body, the outermost expression of creation. The body is matter, inert and impermanent. It is the projected field where the dream-drama of life is played out.

The Illusion of Creation

Though the process of creation appears linear, it is, in truth, an illusory play of light and sound within Consciousness. All phenomena are merely ideas initiated by the "**I AM**." The boundaries and distinctions that seem so real are imaginary constructs. Reality remains unchanged, silently supporting the appearance of this dream-drama. **Reality (underlying Presence, Existence, or Being) or *Parabrahman* alone is real; all else is illusory.**

This understanding is critical for Self-realization, as it shifts the seeker's perspective from identification with the changing forms to recognition of the unchanging Truth.

Key Insights:

1. **Reality Remains Unchanged:**

   Reality does not act, will or think. It simply provides the foundation for all appearances.

2. **The Illusion of Boundaries:**

   The boundaries between these layers—body, mind, ego, and Consciousness — are imaginary. As awareness of Truth arises, these boundaries disappear, leaving only Reality.

3. **Everything is an Appearance:**

   The phenomenal world, with its multiplicity and duality, is nothing more than a play of ideas within Consciousness which itself is a spontaneous appearance on Reality.

4. **The Goal is Awakening:**

   Awakening, or Self-realization, occurs when the illusions of mind, ego, and individuality disappear. What remains is what was always there permanent and unchanged – the underlying Presence, Existence, or Being.

The Path to Self-Realization

Self-realization is the process of awakening by dissolving the illusions of separation and individuality. It is not about attaining something new but about uncovering what has always been present. This journey involves peeling away layers of false identification until only the essence of being remains.

The Process of Realization

In the process of creation, existence (presence or being) first appears to express itself as consciousness, which then identifies with an imaginary ego, shaping an individual sense of self. This ego, in turn, appears to engage with the mind, which constructs thoughts, perceptions, and beliefs. The mind then appears to identify with the body, anchoring the sense of separateness within the material world. However, the path to realization is the reversal of this process. By turning inward, one begins to stop identifying with the imaginary world, body, mind, and ultimately the idea of an ego. On disappearance of ignorance the false identification completely disappears, revealing consciousness in its purest state. From here, what remains is Reality itself—free, limitless, and eternal. This is the essence of Right Understanding, the realization that all distinctions are mere appearances, and the Self has never been separate from the whole.

(World/Body/Mind/Ego) Creation → Consciousness → Reality

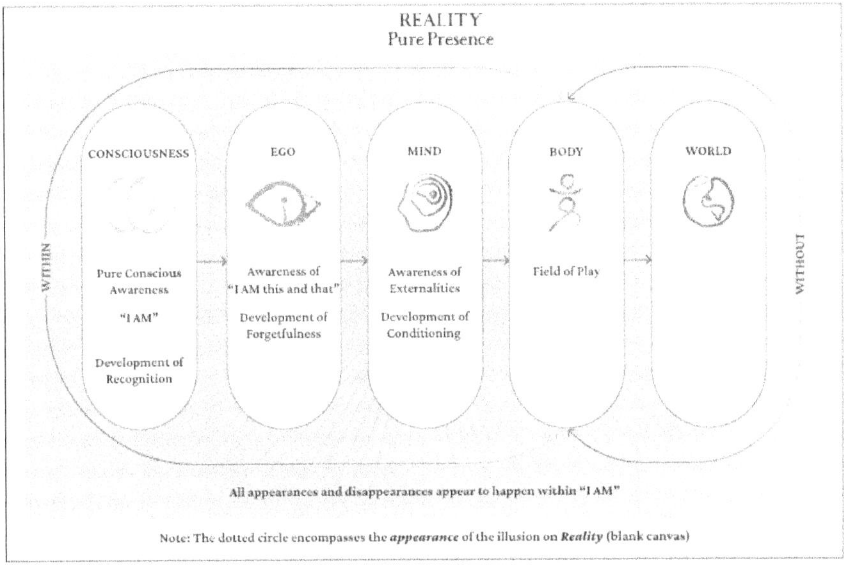

Diagram 4: Reality and the Illusion

1. **Start with Inquiry:**

   Begin by questioning the nature of the world and your identity.

2. **Detach from Form:**

   Recognize that you are not the body or the mind but the awareness observing them.

3. **Anchor in "I AM":**

   Rest in the pure conscious awareness of being, dissolving the idea of separation (ego) and its illusions.

Teachings for Daily Integration

The Truth *(Sat)* offers several practical insights:

1. **Do not take life too seriously and do not take anything personally:**
   Life is a dream-drama, a play of appearances. Recognize its illusory nature and approach it with lightness and humor.
2. **Rest in Stillness:**
   True realization is not found in movement or thought but in stillness. When the mind is silent, the truth of your being naturally reveals itself. Rest in this stillness, for it is the doorway to your true nature.
3. **Detach from Ego:**
   The ego's narratives and attachments are the source of suffering. Let go and return to the simplicity of being.
4. **Live Meditatively:**
   Engage in daily activities with awareness, letting actions flow naturally without thought or analysis.
5. **Return to "I AM":**
   Hold onto the awareness of "**I AM**" as your anchor. This practice dissolves the layers of illusion and eventually reveals the Reality that has always been.

A Journey of Remembering

The above sets the stage for the journey outlined in the Three-Fold Path. The chapters that follow will guide you through Right Understanding, Right Practice, and Right Experience, using the insights of the Truth to help you navigate the layers of existence.

As you walk this path, remember: the Truth you seek is already here. It is not something to attain but something to remember. Let the teachings guide you back to the simplicity and stillness of your true nature.

Introduction

The Three-Fold Path

In silence deep, the journey starts,
A whisper stirs within our hearts.
The path is three, yet truly One,
A way back home, where all is done.

Right Understanding *clears the night,*
Dispelling shadows, bringing light.
It shows the truth beyond the veil,
Where names and forms begin to pale.

Through ***Right Practice****, we start to see,*
The Self that binds, then sets us free.
With non-attachment, we let go,
And feel the quiet currents flow.

Then comes ***Right Experience****, pure and clear,*
The end of seeking, the end of fear.
A timeless state, beyond all thought,
Where peace and joy cannot be sought.

Thus, in the stillness, we arrive,
Awake, aware, fully alive.
The Three-Fold Path, so wise and true,
Leads us back to what we knew.

A journey deep, a simple way,
To know ourselves as light and clay.
In each step taken, truth revealed,
The Self remembered, whole, and healed.

Introduction: Discovering the Three-Fold Path

My journey into the essence of the Three-Fold Path was born from a simple question: *Who am I?* It was a question that would not let go of me. For many years, I sought answers outside of myself—in books, in spiritual teachings, and in the wisdom of others. I wanted to know what it meant to live in peace, to find joy that does not waver, and to experience harmony in every aspect of life. The journey was full of challenges, sometimes humorous, other times deeply transformative. At one point, I thought enlightenment was something I could "achieve" by meditating hard enough or understanding spiritual concepts well enough. I can smile about it now, but back then, I was exhausting myself with effort which became a necessary part of the journey.

As I delved deeper into diverse spiritual teachings and traditions, I came across profound concepts of non-duality, silence, and Self-inquiry. These teachings pointed to a Truth that lay beyond words, something that could only be known through direct experience. But even as I studied, practiced, and meditated, the Truth I sought remained elusive.

Then, one day, it dawned on me: the Truth I sought was not something to be gained, attained or achieved but something to be uncovered. It was already here, as close as my own breath, waiting for me to see it. Peace, joy, and harmony weren't things to be found outside; they were not destinations, but the essence of my own true nature, hidden behind layers of identity, thoughts, beliefs, and fear.

There was once a mountaineer who dreamed of reaching the highest peak. He trained for years, climbing one mountain after another, each one higher than the last. But each time he reached a summit, he felt empty, longing for something more. One day, a wise guide told him, "The peace you seek is not at the summit but within you."

This realization became the foundation of the Three-Fold Path—a path designed not to add more to life, but to help peel away what isn't needed. The path has three essential elements: **Right Understanding, Right Practice, *and* Right Experience.** Together, these form a journey back to the "**I AM**" state of Pure Conscious Awareness, to the awareness that is always present, unchanging, and whole.

The Three-Fold Path isn't about escaping life. It's about fully living, free from the illusion of separateness. It's about seeing clearly, practicing consistently, and experiencing directly. And so, I share this path with you—not as a set of beliefs, but as an invitation to discover the Truth.

The Three-Fold Path: A Simple, Timeless Guide

In an era where information floods our senses and the complexities of modern life create constant inner turmoil, a simple truth remains: peace, joy, and harmony are not to be sought externally but to be discovered within. The Three-Fold Path, a spiritual framework designed to remind and guide us back to our original nature, offers a profound, yet accessible way to realize this truth. This path is not a new invention but a distillation of ancient wisdom, refined through personal experience, practice, and understanding. It provides a roadmap to navigate the journey from confusion to clarity, from individuality to universality, and from suffering to everlasting peace.

A merchant received a treasure map from his father but forgot about it and spent years wandering aimlessly, hoping to stumble upon riches.

One day, he found the map in an old chest and realized it had been with him all along.

The Three-Fold Path is like this map. It doesn't give you treasure but guides you to uncover it within yourself. The principles of **Right Understanding, Right Practice, *and* Right Experience** are simple yet profound directions for discovering the essence of "I AM."

This path isn't about abandoning life's demands or ignoring responsibilities. Instead, it's a way to bring peace, joy, and harmony into every moment by rediscovering what lies at the very core of our being. The Three-Fold Path is timeless, rooted in principles that have guided seekers across cultures and generations.

What is the Three-Fold Path?

At the heart of the Three-Fold Path is the recognition that Truth is non-dual—we are all interconnected, and the divisions we perceive between ourselves and the world are illusory. The teachings invite us to remember that our true nature is timeless, silent, and still, a state that exists beyond the mind's constant chatter. This simple but profound Truth is the foundation of the path.

Through the practice of remembrance, we return again and again to this fundamental Truth. The practice is simple. Truth is supposed to be very simple. We are not striving to attain something new; rather, we are uncovering what has always been within us, the eternal state of Being-Awareness-Bliss ***(Sat-Chit-Ananda – Existence, Consciousness and Bliss or the Ever-Pure Blissful Consciousness)*****.**

1. The path has three interconnected principles. Together, they form a guide to remember and realize our true nature—a nature that is inherently peaceful, joyful, and harmonious.

2. **Right Understanding (Knowing the Truth)** provides right knowledge of the nature of reality and recognizing the "**I AM**" as the essence of ones' being, while teaching us to see through the illusions created by the mind, to recognize the interconnectedness of all life, and to discover the truth beyond our thoughts and perceptions. Learning to see life as it truly is - beyond illusions and ego-driven narratives.

3. **Right Practice (Remembering the Truth)** gives us the tools to ground this understanding in daily life that stabilizes awareness, helping us cultivate habits that nurture inner stillness, clarity, and non-attachment.

4. **Right Experience (Being the Truth)** is the culmination of the path, where we live from a place of peace, joy and unconditional love, seeing ourselves and the world from the perspective of our true nature.

As depicted in image 1 below, The Three-Fold Path emphasizes the dynamic interplay of **Understanding, Practice,** ***and*** **Experience** ***(*****Realization)** *as the foundation for spiritual growth. These principles are not linear steps but a self-reinforcing cycle that deepens progressively.*

Right Understanding provides intellectual clarity about the truth of reality, inspiring the practitioner to engage in Right Practice. Through practice, understanding becomes grounded in experience, leading to glimpses of Realization. These moments of realization, in turn, refine and deepen understanding, creating a continuous feedback loop that leads to the stabilization of awareness in **"I AM."**

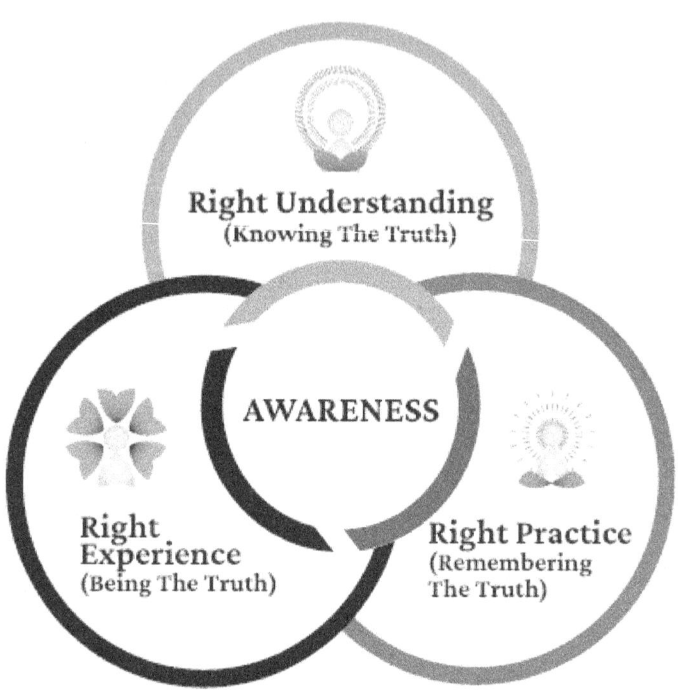

Image 1: The Three-Fold Path

Right Understanding serves as the starting point, offering an intellectual grasp of non-dual truths, such as the impermanence of forms, the ego's illusory nature, and the essence of "**I AM**." This clarity motivates the practitioner to engage deeply in practices like Self-inquiry, meditative abidance, and silence, as they see the purpose and transformative potential of these efforts. Understanding provides a roadmap, helping the seeker navigate the inner journey and overcome doubts. As understanding deepens through study and contemplation, it naturally supports and enriches the practices that follow.

Practice is where intellectual understanding is transformed into lived experience. By engaging in Self-inquiry, meditative abidance, silence, and non-attachment, the practitioner moves beyond theoretical knowledge and begins to embody the teachings. Through consistent practice, moments of realization arise—direct experiences of "**I AM**" that confirm the truth beyond concepts. These glimpses of realization motivate deeper practice, as they provide undeniable evidence of the teachings. Over time, practice becomes less effortful, shifting from a means to an end to a natural expression of one's true nature.

Realization, the direct experiential recognition of one's essence as "**I AM**," is the culmination of understanding and practice. Unlike intellectual knowledge or deliberate effort, realization is effortless and self-evident. It is the recognition of the eternal, unchanging awareness that exists beyond the mind and ego. Each moment of realization strengthens understanding, as the seeker directly perceives truths that were once abstract. These experiences dissolve doubts, refine the seeker's clarity, and further inspire continued practice. Realization also transforms the nature of practice, making it less about "achieving" something and more about resting in the truth that is already present.

The interplay between understanding, practice, and realization creates a self-sustaining cycle. Understanding motivates practice, practice deepens realization, and realization refines understanding, enabling the cycle to repeat at increasingly subtle levels. With each iteration, the practitioner moves closer to a permanent state of realization, where the awareness of **"I AM"** *becomes stable and effortless. At this stage, no further understanding or practice is required. The intellectual frameworks of understanding dissolve as the seeker fully embodies the Truth. Practice becomes redundant, as silence, non-attachment, and surrender are no longer deliberate efforts but natural states of being. Realization becomes constant, unshaken by external circumstances or internal fluctuations.*

Ultimately, the cycle of understanding, practice, and experience culminates in complete liberation. The seeker no longer operates from the level of the ego or intellect but abides fully in the awareness of **"I AM."** *This state is marked by an unwavering peace and freedom, where all striving ceases. This final state represents the fulfillment of the Three-Fold Path, where the seeker, having realized their timeless essence, is no longer a seeker but the boundless awareness they have always been.*

In my own life, each of these steps unfolded gradually. Right Understanding showed me that my true Self was not the thoughts, emotions, or identities I clung to. Right Practice taught me how to let go of attachments and abide in the stillness of awareness. And finally, Right Experience brought the realization that **"I AM"** *is not just a concept but the living, breathing essence of all that is.*

The Three-Fold Path is not a belief system or a set of rigid rules. It's a flexible, practical approach to living in alignment with Truth. This path is not about abandoning life or becoming someone new. It's about uncovering what has always been here. Imagine the vast, open sky. The sky itself is always present—vast, limitless, and untouched. However, clouds may appear, sometimes thick and stormy, other times light and fleeting. These clouds represent thoughts, desires, emotions, identities, and attachments that seem to obscure the sky. Most people identify with the clouds, believing them to be their true nature—constantly shifting, reacting, and changing. But the truth is, no matter how many clouds appear or disappear, the sky itself remains unchanged.

Realizing **"I AM"** *is like shifting awareness away from the clouds and recognizing the ever-present sky. The clouds of ego and mind may come and go, but awareness—the sky—remains still, open, and infinite. When we stop chasing, resisting or identifying with these* *thoughts, desires, emotions, identities, and attachments we naturally abide in the vast, unchanging awareness of* **"I AM."**

Purpose of the Three-Fold Path

The purpose of this path is to dispel the confusion that arises from identifying with the mind, the ego, and the external world. By aligning ourselves with the Truth of who we are—***the Ever-Pure Blissful Consciousness*** — *our lives naturally shift toward greater peace, joy, and harmony. The Three-Fold Path empowers us to transcend the limitations imposed by false identifications and return to a state of perpetual, unchanging joy. The path makes us aware of the unchanging divinity within us all – the divinity that is not an object to be seen but is the underlying unimaginable silent and still force or power in which all manifestations appear and disappear.*

Benefit of the Three-Fold Path

The beauty of this path is its practical application in daily life. Whether navigating personal challenges, relationships, or societal pressures, the Three-Fold Path provides the tools to remain grounded in Truth. As we practice Self-inquiry, meditative abidance, silence, non-attachment, and surrender, we begin to experience life in its purest form, free from the constant push and pull of desires and fears. Eventually, the practice becomes effortless, leading to direct experience of our true nature—one with everything while simultaneously being free from everything.

This book will guide you along each step of the Three-Fold Path. Together, we will explore concepts, reflect on questions, and engage in practices that bring these teachings to life. The journey may challenge certain beliefs or assumptions, but it also promises a transformative return to the simplicity and stillness that define who you truly are.

How to Approach This Book

This book is meant to be more than a read—it's an invitation to explore, question, and experience. As you move through each chapter, take your time with the reflections and exercises. Allow space for remembrance and Self-inquiry and give yourself permission to revisit sections as needed. The Three-Fold Path isn't a race; it's a journey toward clarity, presence, and inner freedom. Remember, this path isn't about achieving enlightenment; it's about realizing the light that's already within you.

Use this book as a guide, a companion in your practice. Keep a journal to capture insights, questions, or realizations that arise along the way. Above all, remember that the Truth you seek is already within you. This path is simply a way to clear away the distractions and return to what you've always known deep inside. So, take your time, be patient, and let the journey unfold!

Chapter 1

Right Understanding
Knowing the Truth

The Light of Right Understanding

A ship adrift in a boundless sea,
Seeks a course, a way to be.
Without the stars to light its way,
The mind will wander, lost astray.

But in the silence, clear and bright,
There burns within a steady light.
No shape, no name, no thought to bind,
A truth beyond the fleeting mind.

Before the roles, before the name,
Before the stories life became,
There is a knowing, deep and still,
A quiet Self, beyond the will.

No separate self, no "I" to claim,
The waves arise, yet are the same.
The ocean moves, yet stays as One,
A dance of light, a burning sun.

We chase the smoke, we fight the haze,
But fanning flames prolong the maze.
Yet when we pause, the winds subside,
And truth emerges, clear inside.

No need to battle, grasp, or chase,
No self to lose, no time, no space.
Just rest and see, let go, be free,
And know, at last, "I AM" is me.

Right Understanding - Knowing the truth

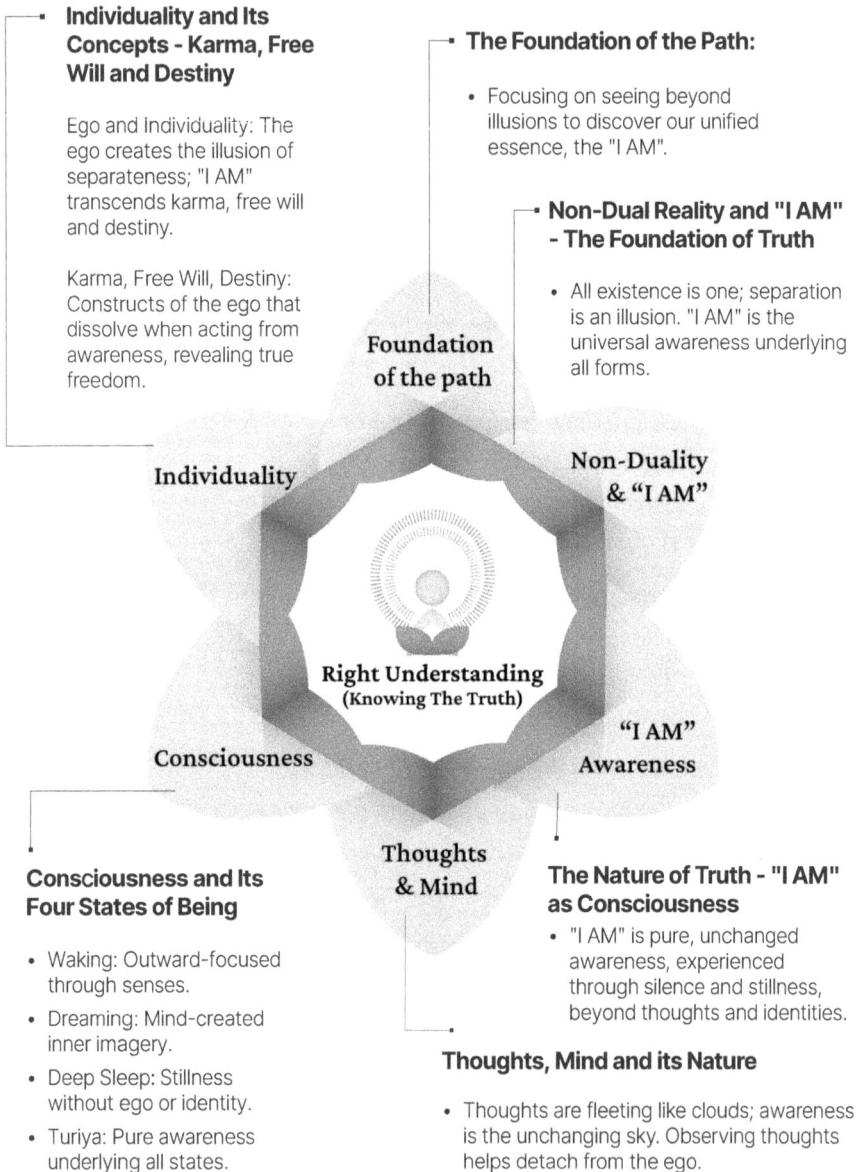

Individuality and Its Concepts - Karma, Free Will and Destiny

Ego and Individuality: The ego creates the illusion of separateness; "I AM" transcends karma, free will and destiny.

Karma, Free Will, Destiny: Constructs of the ego that dissolve when acting from awareness, revealing true freedom.

The Foundation of the Path:

- Focusing on seeing beyond illusions to discover our unified essence, the "I AM".

Non-Dual Reality and "I AM" - The Foundation of Truth

- All existence is one; separation is an illusion. "I AM" is the universal awareness underlying all forms.

Foundation of the path

Individuality

Non-Duality & "I AM"

Right Understanding (Knowing The Truth)

Consciousness

"I AM" Awareness

Thoughts & Mind

Consciousness and Its Four States of Being

- Waking: Outward-focused through senses.
- Dreaming: Mind-created inner imagery.
- Deep Sleep: Stillness without ego or identity.
- Turiya: Pure awareness underlying all states.

The Nature of Truth - "I AM" as Consciousness

- "I AM" is pure, unchanged awareness, experienced through silence and stillness, beyond thoughts and identities.

Thoughts, Mind and its Nature

- Thoughts are fleeting like clouds; awareness is the unchanging sky. Observing thoughts helps detach from the ego.

Diagram 5: Key Concepts Covered in the Chapter

"True understanding is not achieved by analyzing thoughts but by letting go of them. When you stop focusing on the unreal, the Self naturally reveals itself."

"The mind projects confusion by clinging to roles, labels, and stories. Right understanding arises when you see beyond these illusions and recognize the still awareness at the core of your being."

Right Understanding – Knowing the Truth

The Foundation of the Path

Right Understanding is the first step on the Three-Fold Path. Without clear understanding, our journey can feel scattered,like a ship navigating without a compass. Right Understanding comes from having the right knowledge about seeing beyond the illusions of the mind and discovering the truth of who we are. It reveals that at our core, we are not separate individuals but expressions of a single, undivided awareness—the "**I AM**" that exists in all beings. This awareness is not a thought or a concept; it is the direct experience of being. Before you identify as a name, a role, or a body, you are aware of your existence.

When I talk about understanding, I'm not talking about intellectual knowledge or memorizing spiritual concepts. Right Understanding is a deeper knowing, a felt recognition that resonates with your whole being. It's seeing clearly, beyond the filters of the mind, and realizing that your essence is not the roles you play, the thoughts you think, or the experiences you have.

Right Understanding reveals the "**I AM**" as Pure Conscious Awareness—the awareness that is always present, unchanging, and beyond form. This awareness is who you truly are, beneath all the stories and identities you've accumulated over time.

Right Understanding is the foundation of the Three-Fold Path. It's the lens through which we begin to see ourselves and the world more clearly. At its core, Right Understanding is about recognizing that the misunderstanding is that of mistaken identity due to false identifications and that all of what we perceive is filtered through the mind's interpretations, illusions, and attachments. This misunderstanding is in itself imaginary. By seeking to understand the nature of reality beyond these imaginary filters, we begin to glimpse the Truth that underlies all experiences.

In a quiet home, a lamp burned steadily in the corner of a room. Over time, smoke from the lamp began to fill the air, creating a haze that dimmed its light. Concerned, the owner started waving her hands to disperse the smoke, but her efforts only stirred it up further, making the haze worse.

Frustrated, she finally realized that she needed to stop focusing on the smoke and simply let it dissipate naturally. As the air cleared, the light of the lamp shone brightly once again, unobstructed and steady, just as it had always been.

The smoke represents the ego—layers of thoughts, conditioning, and self-identifications—that obscure the truth of "**I AM**." Like the owner, we often attempt to control or eliminate these layers, but our efforts only perpetuate the illusion.

Right Understanding is the realization that you don't need to fight or fix the ego. Instead, by resting in stillness and awareness, the haze of the mind clears naturally, allowing the light of your true Self to shine unobstructed. In that moment, we realize that our true Self was never lost—just momentarily obscured.

Section 1

Non-Dual Reality and "I AM" – The Foundation of Truth

"All that exists is One, and this One is awareness itself."

"You are not separate from that which pervades all things. Like space, it is within and beyond, untouched yet ever-present. This supreme, non-dual Reality is not something to reach—it is what you already are."

Waves of One Ocean

From the crest of the wave to the calm of the sea,
What seems apart is unity to me.
Each ripple, each motion, a dance of the whole,
No boundary exists in the ocean of the soul.

"I AM" is the thread that weaves through all,
Through joy and despair, through rise and fall.
Not separate, not distant, no "other" to find,
Just the light of awareness in all humankind.

Like the wave and the ocean, distinct yet the same,
We forget the vastness, caught in the name.
But when we dissolve the illusion, let go of the strife,
We find in the One, the true essence of life.

So let go of the barriers, the judgments, the view,
For the truth is eternal: there's no "me" or "you."
Only Oneness remains, pure, ever free,
The infinite boundless, where "I AM" will always be.

One of the greatest challenges we face is the belief in separation. We see ourselves as distinct individuals navigating a world filled with "others." This perception creates conflict, fear, and the constant need to protect or enhance our ego. But this sense of separation is an illusion.

Non-duality is a concept that can sound abstract, but in essence, it's profoundly simple: everything is One. There is no other. There is no true separation between you, me, and the world around us. We are all expressions of the same underlying awareness, manifesting in different forms. This conscious awareness or existence is what I call "**I AM**."

Imagine the ocean: from the shore, we see individual waves, each with its own form and motion. But if we look closer, we realize that every wave is simply an expression of the ocean. Each wave rises, peaks, and dissolves back into the water, yet it was never separate from the ocean to begin with. In the same way, each of us is like a wave on the ocean of existence. Our individual forms are temporary expressions of a single, boundless Awareness.

One of the most profound understandings that Right Understanding brings is the recognition of non-duality, the idea that all of existence is one indivisible whole. Non-dual reality suggests that the divisions we see—between self and other, between objects and people, between success and failure—are ultimately illusions. Beneath these apparent separations lies a singular, unified field of existence or awareness.

Non-dual reality invites us to see beyond surface distinctions and recognize the unity that underlies all forms. This understanding can be both liberating and challenging. It asks us to let go of rigid identities, judgments, and attachments, which often create a sense of separation and conflict. When we begin to see ourselves and others as interconnected parts of a larger whole, compassion and empathy naturally arise. We are no longer isolated; we are deeply, inherently one with all of life.

Reflection Exercise: Embracing Unity

Take a few moments to reflect on a time when you felt a profound sense of connection with others, nature, or the world around you. Perhaps it was during a quiet walk in nature, a shared moment of laughter, or a time of giving and receiving kindness. As you recall this experience, notice how it feels in your body and mind. Let yourself sink into that sense of unity, allowing it to dissolve any feelings of isolation or separation. This is a taste of non-dual reality—a reminder that beneath all appearances, we are already whole and one.

Section 2

The Nature of Truth – "I AM" as Consciousness

"**I AM**" is the foundation of all experience, unchanging and eternal."

"Anchor yourself unwaveringly in the awareness of '**I AM**.' This is both the starting point and the final realization—where all seeking begins and where it ultimately dissolves."

The Stillness of "I AM"

Beneath the storm of thought and tide of care,
Lies a silence untouched, always there.
Not bound by the roles that come and fade,
Nor by the shadows the mind has made.

"I AM," the essence, the unshaken ground, In
its quiet, eternal presence, we're found. Like a
mirror that re lects, yet stays pristine, A
witness untouched by the world it's seen.

No name can bind it, no form contain,
It watches the joy, the sorrow, the pain.

Understanding "I AM" - Consciousness

Resting Naturally (Without Movement)

Pure Conscious Awareness (Self)

Silence

Still

Undisturbed

Peace (Bliss)

Unconditioned

Unidentified

Unlimited

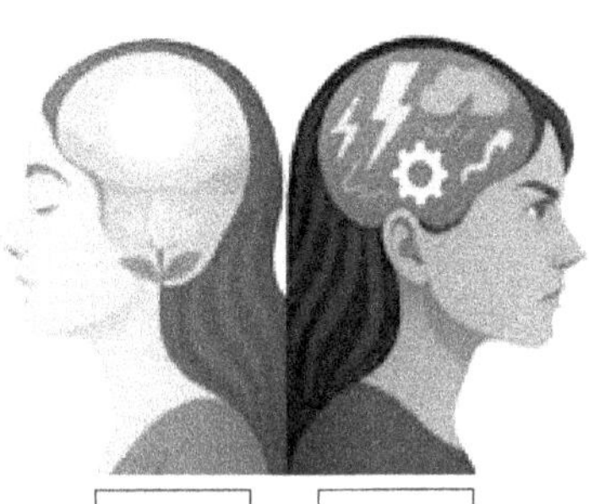

Quiet Mind

Active Mind

Dreaming/ Active Projecting (With Movement)

Sensory Awarness (Ego)

False Identification

Ego Driven

Attachments

Condtitioned

Identified

Limited

"I AM," is the bridge between illusion and truth - It is the purest sense of being before the mind imposes labels, identities, or roles. When attention remains in "I AM," the mind's distractions dissolve, revealing the silent awareness that has always been present.

The mind projects, but awareness remains unchanged - When the mind turns outward, it constructs a world of thoughts, emotions, and identities. When it turns inward, these projections fade, allowing one to abide in the unchanging awareness that is beyond all states of waking, dreaming, and deep sleep.

"I AM" is Pure Conscious Awareness or Consciousness, but not the ultimate Reality (Pure Presence) - While "I AM" represents Self-awareness, it is still within the realm of duality. The final transcendence occurs when even "I AM" dissolves, revealing Reality itself- formless, limitless, and beyond even the subtlest identification.

Identification creates limitation - The moment "I AM" is attached to a thought, role, or concept (e.g., "I AM this" or "I AM that"), it becomes conditioned and limited. Letting go of these identifications allows one to rest in pure being, beyond the fluctuations of the mind.

Silence and stillness are the key to realization - The Truth cannot be grasped through intellectual effort. It is revealed in the absence of mental noise. When the mind is quiet and free from movement, the Self naturally shines forth as the only reality.

Image 2: Understanding "I AM"

Beyond the chatter, the stories, the strife,
It holds the secret of all that is life.

Sit by its stillness, let it unfold,
This truth that's ancient, yet ever untold.
For in the silence, the eternal flame,
Burns bright and steady, beyond a name.

What is "I AM"?

At the heart of Right Understanding lies a simple truth: *You are not your thoughts, roles, or identities.* These are temporary layers that come and go, but beneath them is the unchanging Pure Conscious Awareness or Consciousness of "**I AM**." This "**I AM**" is not personal; it is the same in all beings. It is the silent awareness that observes your thoughts, feels your emotions, and experiences your life.

The Truth in the Three-Fold Path is not about beliefs or opinions; it's about recognizing the reality that is timeless, unchanging, and ever-present. This Truth is often described as silent and still, existing beyond the mind's interpretations and narratives. It's the essence that remains permanent, no matter how thoughts and emotions fluctuate.

However, there is a subtle but profound distinction between "**I AM**" (Pure Conscious Awareness) and Reality (Pure Presence). The "**I AM**" is conscious awareness of pure being and the doorway to the ultimate Truth. Yet even this "**I AM**" is within the realm of duality. Reality, or the Absolute, is beyond even the sense of "**I AM**." It is formless, boundless, and beyond all distinctions. When even the "**I AM**" dissolves, what remains is Reality itself—pure existence, beyond experience, beyond consciousness, beyond all knowing.

The "**I AM**" that I speak of is not an identity in the usual sense. It is the conscious awareness that is present before any thought, feeling, or belief. Think of it like a mirror: a mirror reflects everything that comes before it, but it is untouched by what it reflects. The "**I AM**" is this mirror-like awareness. It is not affected by the images that appear within it, yet it illuminates everything. By resting in the awareness of "**I AM**," you begin to see that everything else-- thoughts, emotions, identities—arises within it but does not define it.

However, just as the mirror is still an object reflecting light, the "**I AM**" is still a subtle state of experience. To go beyond the "**I AM**" is to transcend all experience and rest in the Reality that neither reflects nor is reflected. The "**I AM**" is the doorway—Reality is what remains once you pass through it.

Ancient sages have pointed to silence as the embodiment of Truth. Ramana Maharshi, a renowned teacher of non-dual wisdom and my guide, famously stated, **"Silence is truth, stillness is God."** In this sense, Truth isn't something that can be spoken or written; it's something we experience directly, in moments of pure conscious awareness.

Imagine sitting by a lake at dawn. The water is perfectly still, mirroring the sky without distortion. In the same way, when the mind is quiescent or silent, it reflects the Truth within us without interference. This silence reveals a state of pure presence, where we are not defined by thoughts or identities but simply are!

But just as the reflection in the water is not the sky itself, the "**I AM**" is not the final Reality—it is the last point before the final dissolution into the infinite. To go beyond, one must let go even of this sense of being, of "**I AM**," and merge into that which has no name, no state, and no distinction.

Contemplative Practice: Sitting with Silence

Set aside ten to fifteen minutes each day to sit in silence. Find a quiet space, close your eyes, and allow thoughts to come and go without engaging with them. Notice the silence that exists between thoughts—the space of awareness that remains unaffected by whatever arises in the mind. This is a practice of meeting Truth as it is, beyond interpretation.

Section 3

Thoughts, Mind, and its Nature

"Thoughts are like clouds; they pass by, but they don't define the sky."

"Allow whatever arises to arise and whatever departs to depart. Do not resist or grasp. Simply rest in awareness and see what remains unchanged."

The Sky Beyond the Clouds

The mind is a river, a restless stream,
Casting reflections, weaving a dream.
Its chatter unending, its stories so loud,
But thoughts are just shadows, like passing clouds.

The sky remains, vast and clear,
Unchanged by the storms that may appear.
Each thought a whisper, a fleeting show,
What comes, let it come; what goes, let it go.

For you are the stillness, the watcher unseen,
The space where the clouds drift, serene.
Not bound by the stories, the fears, or the past,
You are the essence, eternal and vast.

So sit in the silence, let the mind play,
Its dance of illusions will soon fade away.
In the gaps between thoughts, a truth will arise,
The pure light of awareness, unclouded skies.

The mind (an aggregate of thoughts) is a powerful tool, capable of forming complex thoughts, analyzing information, and imagining future possibilities. But the mind can also obscure reality by projecting assumptions, judgments, and fears onto our experiences. Right Understanding includes recognizing the transient nature of thoughts and learning to observe them without attachment.

I like to compare the mind to a talkative friend who never stops chattering. Thoughts are constantly popping up, one after another, each one vying for our attention. But just because a thought arises doesn't mean we have to identify with it. Thoughts are like clouds drifting across the sky. They may obscure the sky for a moment, but they don't change the nature of the sky itself. In the same way, thoughts may obscure our awareness, but they don't change the essence of who we are— the ***Ever-Pure Blissful Consciousness***. This awareness is our true nature—unmoved by the mind's fluctuations.

If we were to listen to our minds all day, it would be like watching a reality TV show with endless plot twists, drama, and opinions. The mind loves to be the star of its own show, but awareness is the silent observer, watching the show without getting entangled.

When we begin to observe thoughts rather than identify with them, a shift occurs. We realize that we are not our thoughts;

we are the space in which thoughts arise. This shift frees us from being controlled by the mind's habitual patterns and reactions, allowing us to experience life with greater clarity and equanimity.

Guided Practice: Watching Thoughts Like Clouds

Spend ten to fifteen minutes observing your thoughts as though they are clouds passing across the sky. Sit comfortably, close your eyes, and bring your attention to the flow of thoughts. Imagine each thought as a cloud, drifting across the sky of your awareness. Avoid following or analyzing any thought; simply notice it, then let it go. As you practice this, you may find moments of stillness between thoughts—these are glimpses of the silent, spacious awareness that lies beneath the mind.

Section 4

Consciousness and Its Four States of Being

"Awareness is permanent, while states change."

"Through waking, dream, and deep sleep, the sense of being remains unchanged, while the individual self and the world continuously shift. The body and external reality are temporary appearances, fleeting like images on a screen. But the screen itself—the pure awareness of being—is eternal and unchanging."

The Fourfold Journey of Awareness

In waking light, the senses call,
We dance in the world, believing it all.
Through sights and sounds, we weave the day,
Yet "I AM" watches, still and gray.

In dreams, we wander through shadowed
lands, With fears and hopes shaped by mind's
hands. The fleeting stories, the inner disguise,
Yet "I AM" lingers, beyond the skies.

In deep sleep's hush, no thoughts arise,
The ego fades, no "self" survives.
A stillness profound, a silent domain,
Where "I AM" rests, untouched by the strain.

And then there's Turiya, the truth revealed,
The constant flame no veil can conceal.
It's not a state, but the essence of all,
Pure awareness, answering the call.

Four states unfold, yet only one stays,
The witness eternal, through nights and days.
In knowing this truth, we find our release,
A timeless embrace, a boundless peace.

To understand ourselves more deeply, it helps to explore the layers of consciousness. According to ancient teachings, consciousness has four states: **waking, dreaming, deep sleep,** ***and*** **Turiya,** *often described as pure conscious awareness. Each state reveals a unique aspect of our awareness and how we perceive reality.*

1. **Waking State**: This is the state we are most familiar with—interacting with the world, engaging with others, and carrying out daily tasks. In the waking state, our awareness is directed

outward through the senses, and we identify strongly withour body and mind. It's where we experience physical phenomena as "real." However, even here, the "**I AM**" is present, silently observing.

2. **Dreaming State**: In the dreaming state, our awareness withdraws from the physical senses and instead engages with the mind's inner imagery. Dreams feel vivid and real while we're experiencing them, yet they are composed of memories, desires, and unconscious impressions. The dreaming state shows us how our mind creates experiences based on its own internal reality, often shaped by emotions, fears, and hopes. But behind every dream, "**I AM**" remains as the unchanging witness.

3. **Deep Sleep State**: Deep sleep is a state of rest without dreams or mental activity. In deep sleep, we experience a profound sense of peace and rejuvenation. There is no ego, no identity, no conflict—only an undisturbed stillness. Though we are not consciously aware in this state, deep sleep gives us a glimpse of a reality beyond the mind. It's a space of pure rest, where our awareness exists without form or content. This awareness is "**I AM.**"

4. **Turiya (Pure Conscious Awareness)**: Turiya, sometimes referred to as "the fourth state," is a state of pure conscious awareness that exists beyond waking, dreaming, and deep sleep. It is a state where "**I AM**" stands alone, free from identification with the body, mind, or any form. Turiya represents our true essence, the awareness that is always present, undisturbed, and beyond any experiences. Turiya is not a state in the same sense as the others; rather, it's an underlying reality that remains constant, regardless of which state we're in. Pure Conscious Awareness is always available to us, and realizing it brings a profound sense of peace, unity, and clarity.

Exercise: Observing States of Consciousness

Throughout your day, take a few moments to observe your current state of awareness. When you're fully awake, notice the engagement of your senses and how you interact with the physical world. If you recall a dream, consider the dream's vividness and emotional impact. In the evening, reflect on your experience of deep sleep. Each morning, try to remember how you felt upon waking from a restful night's sleep.

As you practice this observation, allow yourself to recognize the presence of awareness beneath each state. Turiya is always there, even if it feels subtle. With practice, you'll start to notice glimpses of this underlying awareness, revealing a space of peace and presence within you.

Section 5

Individuality and its concepts – Karma, Free Will, and Destiny

"The notion or appearance of individuality is an illusory experience within awareness, not separate from it."

"The sense of individuality is the veil that creates the illusion of separation from the Divine. When this illusion dissolves, what remains is not 'you' realizing God, but the direct recognition that you were never anything but That."

The Illusion of "me"

A name, a face, a fleeting part,
The ego we wear, the mind's fine art.
A role in the drama, a mask we don,
Yet beneath it all, the Self shines on.

Like a snake mistaken on a twilight rope,
The ego deceives, offering false hope.
We cling to its whispers, its fears, its pride,
Yet the truth of "I AM" resides inside.

Karma spins its wheel, life takes its flow,
Free will seems to guide where we go.
But step back and see, the dance is one,
The doer dissolves, the illusion undone.

Destiny's threads weave stories we claim,
But the tapestry's source is forever the same.
Not bound by the lines of what seems to be,
In "I AM," we find infinite unity.

Lay down the mask, let the drama cease,
What's left is presence, eternal peace.
No more the actor, no more the stage,
Only pure awareness, beyond time and age.

Understanding Ego: The illusion of Individuality

A central part of Right Understanding is recognizing the illusory nature of individuality. Self-realization is not about trying to dissolve the ego or individuality; it is to make you realize that it was never there in the first place.

Take the example of the mind misidentifying a rope to be a snake. The rope appears to be a snake as long as the mind identifies with the rope being the snake. But once the truth is seen or understood, the false knowledge that it is a snake disappears (along with all the emotions and attributes related to the snake) but not the snake itself for it was never there in the first place.

The ego is the false sense of self, operating through the mind to define itself as a separate entity. It clings to roles, achievements, and identities, building a fragile sense of self. But the ego is not the real you. It is a shadow cast by the mind. Ask yourself: *Who were you before you were given a name?* The answer points to the pure conscious awareness of "**I AM**," unburdened by labels and roles.

We often view ourselves as distinct, separate individuals, defined by our experiences, choices, and beliefs. However, this individual self, or ego, is a construct shaped by thought patterns, memories, and conditioning. True freedom lies in understanding and transcending the limits of this individual identity. Individuality is a limited perspective created by the mind. It is like a role in a play, a mask we wear for a time. Beneath this role lies the truth of "**I AM**," which is universal, unchanging, and shared by all beings.

Remember always that our true Self is not bound by the appearance of ego's limitations. Just as actors remove their costumes after a performance, we can practice setting aside our individual identities and rest in the awareness of "**I AM**." In this awareness, we experience a profound connection to all of life, realizing that each of us is a unique expression of the same consciousness.

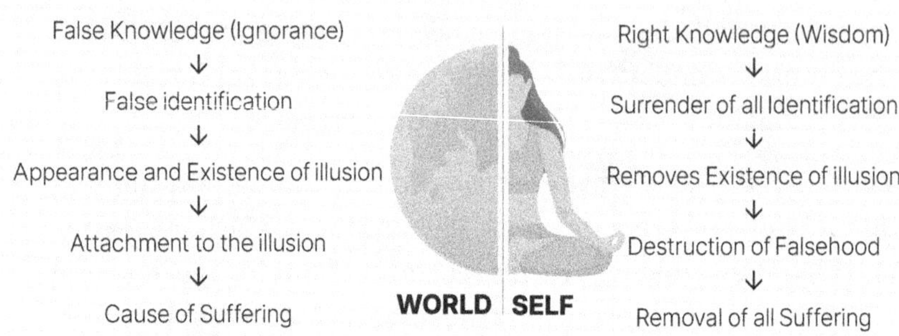

The Rope and the Snake (Illusion of Fear):

- When seen in dim light, a rope might be mistaken for a snake. Fear and panic arise from this false identification.
- Once right knowledge reveals it as a rope, the illusion vanishes instantly. Similarly, ignorance gives rise to false perceptions that cloud the truth of reality.

The Dream World (Illusion of Experience):

- In a dream, we experience vivid sights, sounds, and emotions that feel completely real. Yet, upon waking, we realize that none of it ever existed.
- This illustrates how ignorance creates a false sense of reality. In truth, our~awareness (knowledge) remains unchanged through both waking and dream states.

The Movie Screen and Characters (Illusion of Identity):

- The screen in a movie remains constant and unchanged, even as characters and dramatic events unfold on it. We may become emotionally involved with these characters, forgetting that they are fictional.
- Likewise, in life, ignorance makes us identify with fleeting roles and experiences, obscuring the awareness (screen) that is ever-present and unchanging.

The Mirage in the Desert (illusion of Desire):

- A thirsty traveler in the desert may see a mirage of water. Though the water appears real, it vanishes upon closer inspection, leaving only barren sand.
- Ignorance creates illusions of fulfillment through external desires, but right knowledge reveals that real peace and happiness are found within, not through the mirage of worldly pursuits.

Image 3: Right Knowledge vs. False Knowledge

Exercise: Practice of Observing the Ego in Light of "I AM"

*Ego Watch: Spend a day observing when and how the ego arises. Notice when you feel the need to defend, prove, or enhance your sense of self. Remind yourself that these impulses are expressions that define the ego, not your true Self. Bring your awareness back to "***I AM***," the silent observer behind these impulses. Over time, this practice loosens the concept of an ego, allowing you to experience greater freedom and unity.*

In the Three-Fold Path, individuality is seen as a tool that serves us but does not define us (it is treated as a functional entity in the dream drama of life). Here, we explore some aspects of individuality that contribute to our sense of self: **karma, free will**, and **destiny**.

Karma

Karma is often understood as the law of cause and effect: thoughts, intentions, and actions create effects that influence future experiences. Many seekers struggle with the concept of karma. We wonder, *Am I bound by my past actions? Do I have free will?* The answers lie in understanding our true nature.

Karma operates at the level of the mind and body, not at the level of awareness. When we identify with the ego, we feel bound by karma because we see ourselves as the doer of actions. But when we realize that our true Self is the silent witness of actions rather than the doer, karma loses its grip and we see karma for what it is: a natural process of cause and effect – actions arise, consequences follow, but you remain free. Awareness remains untouched by it.

"True freedom is not found in external circumstances but in releasing the false sense of doership. When the illusion of personal action dissolves, what remains is effortless being—action happens, but there is no 'one' claiming to act." This is not about escaping action but about acting without attachment. When we act from awareness, our actions flow naturally, untainted by ego.

Exercise: Observing Karma in Action

Throughout your day, observe how your actions create effects—both immediately and in the days that follow. Notice how a kind gesture affects others and how negative emotions may impact your interactions. Practicing awareness of karma can help you choose actions that align with peace and joy, contributing to a life of greater harmony.

Practice Insight:

When faced with a challenging situation, pause and ask yourself, "Who is experiencing this? Am I the one reacting, or am I the one observing?" This simple question shifts your perspective from the ego to the awareness of **"I AM."**

Free Will

Free will is the experience of choice. We feel that we can make decisions and influence our lives through our actions. On one level, free will appears to be real—it allows us to make choices that shape our growth, relationships, and experiences. But on a deeper level, free will is limited by our conditioning, beliefs, and desires. The choices we make often come from patterns formed over time rather than true freedom.

The Three-Fold Path invites us to look beyond conditioned free will and explore a deeper form of freedom. When we act from our essence—rather than ego-based desires—we make choices that align with peace, love, and truth. In this way, free will transforms from a limited experience to a means of expressing our true nature.

> ***Reflection on Free Will***
>
> *Take a moment to reflect on a recent decision. Ask yourself: What motivated this choice? Was it driven by ego (personal desires or fears), or did it arise from a deeper sense of peace and clarity? By examining the motivations behind our actions, we begin to understand when we are operating from conditioned patterns versus a place of true freedom.*

Destiny

Destiny refers to life circumstances, events, and experiences that unfold seemingly beyond our control. Many spiritual traditions suggest that certain aspects of our life are "pre-determined" by the natural flow of existence. For example, our birth, family, and specific challenges may be part of our destiny, shaping us in unique ways.

However, understanding destiny on the Three-Fold Path means seeing it not as a rigid plan but as an unfolding journey. Destiny provides opportunities for growth, awakening, and realization. Rather than resisting our life circumstances, we can learn to embrace them as part of the path. This attitude frees us from the struggle of trying to "control" life, allowing us to experience greater harmony and trust in the natural flow.

Reflection on Destiny

Consider an event in your life that felt beyond your control. Reflect on how it shaped you and what it taught you. Instead of viewing it as something that happened "to you," try seeing it as something that happened "for you." This perspective shift allows you to embrace destiny as part of your unique journey.

In the Three-Fold Path, karma, free will, and destiny are understood as constructs that govern the realm of the ego and mind, but they hold no sway over the true Self. The validity of karmic laws is only applicable as long as false identification with the body and mind continues. At this level, life appears as a series of preordained activities and experiences determined by past actions, all orchestrated by a personal God (Ishwara or the "**I AM**" God), who administers the consequences of karma. Free will, in this instance, seems limited to the choice of realizing the Self—a realization that dissolves the illusion of separation and, with it, the relevance of karma. Once the Self is realized, the sense of personal doership disappears, leaving no one to act, experience, or bear consequences. The laws of karma, destiny, and even Ishwara's jurisdiction become redundant, as they pertain only to the illusory realm of individuality. In the state of pure conscious awareness, actions arise spontaneously, untainted by attachment or identity, reflecting the effortless harmony of the Absolute.

Summary: The Nature of Individuality

In this exploration of individuality, we see that karma, free will, and destiny are aspects of the personal self—tools that help us navigate life, learn, and grow. Yet, they do not define or have any effect on our true nature. The Three-Fold Path teaches us to appreciate these aspects without becoming attached to them. By recognizing their limitations, we begin to see ourselves as more than the sum of our experiences and choices. We begin to glimpse a freedom that lies beyond the ego, beyond conditioned patterns, and beyond the idea of a "separate self."

As we move forward to the next chapter, **Right Practice**, we'll explore ways to anchor this understanding through daily practices. By cultivating Self-inquiry, meditative abidance, silence, non-attachment, and surrender, we build a foundation for abiding in the true Self—a Self that is free, peaceful, and deeply connected to all of life.

This concludes Chapter 1: Right Understanding. We've covered the following core ideas:

- ***Non-Dual Reality:***

  The Truth is non-dual. Recognizing the oneness of all existence.

- ***The Nature of Truth:***

  Understanding Truth as silence and stillness, beyond the mind's fluctuations.

- ***Thoughts and Mind:***

  Observing thoughts without attachment, revealing a deeper awareness.

- ***Consciousness and Its Four States:***

  Exploring waking, dreaming, deep sleep, and Turiya (Pure Consciousness).

- ***Individuality – Karma, Free Will, and Destiny:***

  Embracing these concepts as part of life's journey while looking beyond them to find true freedom.

Exercises for Right Understanding

- **Tracing Thoughts to the Source**

  Sit quietly and observe your thoughts. For each thought, ask, "To whom does this thought occur?" Let this question lead you back to the awareness of **"I AM."**

- **Recognizing the Witness**

  Spend a few minutes each day observing your emotions. Notice that while emotions come and go, the awareness observing them remains constant.

Chapter 2

Right Practice
Remembering the Truth

The Path of Right Practice

To act in truth, to live in light,
To rest in Self, serene and bright.
Not through struggle, not through force,
But through return to the silent Source.

The sculptor carves, removing stone,
Revealing what was always known.
So too we strip illusion's veil,
Until the light within prevails.

Who am I?*—the question calls,*
Breaking down the ego's walls.
Not this, not that, not form nor name,
Only the formless, vast and same.

The river flows, it does not try,
Yet reaches oceans, deep and wide.
Right Practice asks for no control,
Just quiet rest within the Whole.

Be still, be here, let go, be free,
Truth is found in simply Be.
No grasping mind, no path to roam,
For "I AM" is the only home.

Right Practice - Remembering the truth

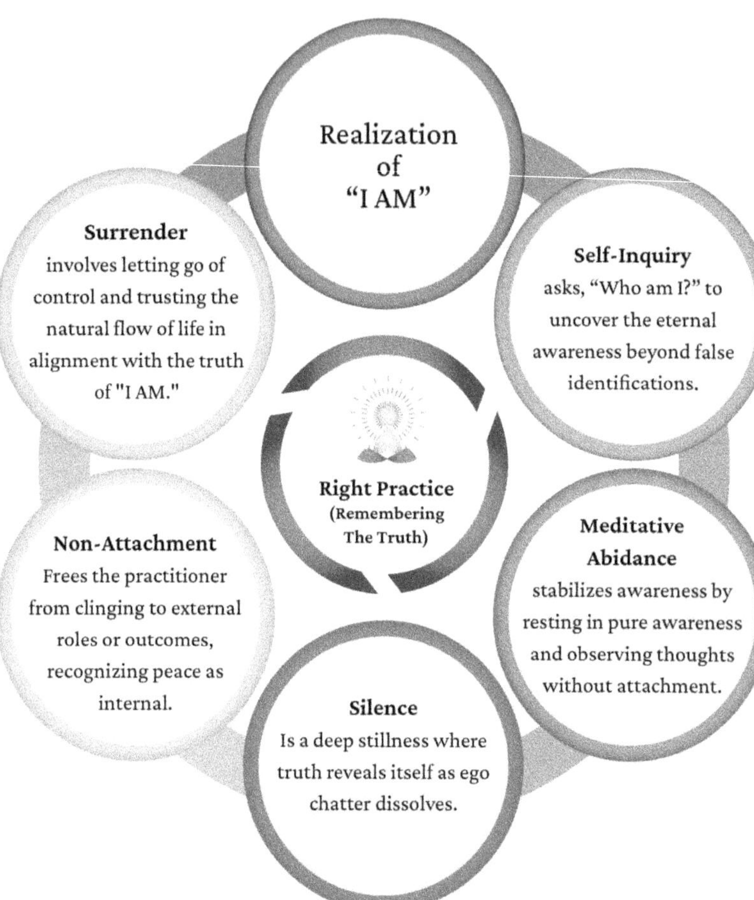

Realization
of
“I AM”
Surrender
involves letting go of
control and trusting the
natural flow of life in
alignment with the truth
of "I AM."
Self-Inquiry
asks, “Who am I?” to
uncover the eternal
awareness beyond false
identifications.
Right Practice
(Remembering
The Truth)
Non-Attachment
Frees the practitioner
from clinging to external
roles or outcomes,
recognizing peace as
internal.
Meditative
Abidance
stabilizes awareness by
resting in pure awareness
and observing thoughts
without attachment.
Silence
Is a deep stillness where
truth reveals itself as ego
chatter dissolves.

> Right Practice integrates understanding and experience of **"I AM"** through interconnected practices, leading to peace and inner freedom.

Unified Experience:

> Over time, Self-inquiry, meditative abidance, silence, non-attachment, and surrender blend into a seamless experience.

> Effort dissolves into a natural state of being where silence and surrender become expressions of the realized Self.

The practitioner lives with peace, joy, and freedom, unburdened by ego or control.

Diagram 6: Key Concepts Covered in the Chapter

"Right Practice is not about effort or control; it is the quiet resting in awareness, allowing truth to reveal itself."

"True action flows naturally, like a river reaching the ocean—not through force, but by surrendering to the One."

Right Practice – Remembering the Truth

"To perform any action for '**I AM**' to realize '**I AM**' is Right Action
To meditate on '**I AM**' to realize '**I AM**' is Right Meditation
To ask the question 'Who am I?' to realize '**I AM**' is Right Wisdom
To surrender to '**I AM**' to realize '**I AM**' is Right Devotion"

Abidance in "I AM"

Right Practice is about stabilizing awareness in "**I AM**". It's one thing to understand our true nature intellectually; it's another to experience and live from it consistently. Right Practice provides the tools that help us ground the knowledge of "**I AM**" in daily life, anchoring us in the present moment, free from attachments and identifications.

It is the bridge between understanding and experience. While understanding helps us recognize the nature of reality, practice grounds that understanding in daily life, allowing it to become our lived reality. Right Practice invites us to engage in simple yet profound activities that bring us back to the present moment, fostering inner stability and freeing us from attachment to thoughts, desires, and outcomes.

A sculptor worked tirelessly to carve a statue from a massive block of marble. People marveled at his skill, but he simply smiled and said, "I am not creating anything. I am only removing what doesn't belong."

Right Practice is like this sculptor's work. Through it, we strip away the layers of ego, revealing the awareness of "**I AM**." The process requires patience and persistence, but with each practice, a little more of your true nature shines through.

This chapter explores key practices that support us in stabilizing awareness and abiding in a state of peace. Through practices like **Self-inquiry, meditative abidance, silence, non-attachment, and surrender**, we deepen our connection to the Truth within, ultimately allowing us to live from a place of inner clarity and harmony.

Section 1

Self-Inquiry and "I AM" - The Core Practice

"The question 'Who am I?' peels away all that '**I AM**' not."

"Let go of all inquiries except one: 'Who am I?' The only undeniable truth is that you exist. The certainty lies in '**I AM**,' but any identification beyond that—'**I AM** this' or '**I AM** that'—is merely a construct of the mind. Seek to discover what you are beyond all labels, and '**I AM**' will reveal itself."

The Question That Unveils

Who am I, this question I breathe,
A silent echo beneath the sheath.
Layer by layer, I begin to see,
The false identities unravel from me.

I am not the roles, the labels, the name,
Not the victories won, nor the fleeting fame.
Not the body that moves, nor the mind that schemes,
Not the fleeting stories, nor the transient dreams.

Who am I, I ask, with every layer torn,
The light of awareness begins to be born.
No words can answer, no thought can stay,
Only "I AM" remains, unmarked by the fray.

A presence eternal, vast and clear,
Free from the shadows of doubt and fear.
No longer confined by "this" or "that,"
I rest in the truth, where the ego shat (shattered).

Peel away the false, and there you'll find,
The essence unchanging, beyond the mind.
Ask it again, let the illusion cease,
"Who am I?" whispers the voice of peace.

Self-inquiry is a practice that goes directly to the heart of spiritual exploration. If there is one practice that transforms and transcends the ego and mind, it is **Self-inquiry**. This simple question—*"Who am I?"*—when asked with deep intensity and conviction has the power to dissolve the ego and reveal the awareness behind it. But Self-inquiry is not about finding a verbal answer. It's about turning the mind inward, tracing every thought back to its source. The purpose of Self-inquiry is to peel away layers of identification with thoughts, roles, and beliefs until we arrive at the awareness of "**I AM**."

It is like peeling away layers of an onion, each layer representing a belief or identity you hold about yourself. As you remove each layer—"**I AM** a professional," "**I AM** a parent," "**I AM** a thinker"—you eventually arrive at the core of your being, the simple and profound awareness of "**I AM**."

Imagine you're playing a game where each label you drop brings you closer to a treasure. Every time you let go of an identity, you get closer to finding the treasure of your true Self. But here's the twist—the treasure was always right there. It was just buried under all those labels.

Guided Practice: Who Am I?

1. Find a comfortable seated position, close your eyes, and take a few deep breaths.
2. Begin by asking yourself, "Who am I?" Let the question settle in your mind without forcing an answer.
3. As thoughts arise, notice them without judgment. If you find yourself thinking, "**I AM** a person," or "**I AM** my thoughts," gently set these ideas aside and return to the question.
4. Repeat the question quietly to yourself, allowing it to dissolve surface-level identities and bring you to a place of inner silence.
5. With practice, you may experience moments of pure awareness—where the answer to "Who am I?" is simply the silent awareness of "**I AM**."

This practice is powerful and can be revisited regularly. The goal isn't to arrive at a specific answer but to reach a state of awareness where you recognize yourself as Consciousness itself, beyond any particular identity.

Reflection on the "I AM"

After each Self-inquiry session, spend a few minutes reflecting on any insights or experiences that arose. How did it feel to ask "Who am I?" without attaching an answer? What did you discover about your sense of self? Record these reflections in a journal to track your inner journey over time.

Contemplative Practice: Resting in "I AM"

Sit comfortably with your eyes closed and ask yourself, "Who am I, without any labels?" Let go of each thought, role, or story that comes up. Allow yourself to rest in the simple awareness of ***"I AM,"*** *feeling the peace that arises when you don't have to be anyone or achieve anything.*

Section 2

Meditative Abidance in "I AM"

"Meditation is not the act of becoming; it is the art of remembering. In stillness, the '**I AM**' shines forth, unclouded by thought or identity. Rest here, at the center of your being, and you will find that the peace you seek was never outside—it was always within, waiting in silence to be noticed."

"Resting in the pure awareness of '**I AM**' is true samadhi. It is the effortless state of simply being, free from all labels and identifications like '**I AM** this' or '**I AM** that.' When the mind no longer clings to these false associations, what remains is the boundless, unshaken presence of your true nature."

The Stillness Within

In the quiet, the whispers fade,
No need to seek, no effort made.
The breath flows softly, a gentle tide,
Drawing me inward where truths abide.

The thoughts arise, like clouds in the sky,
Transient shapes, they drift and die.
I am not the storm, nor the fleeting breeze,
But the silent vastness that sees with ease.

No need to control, no need to bind,
The peace I seek is already mine.
In the "I AM," the center, the core,
Lies the presence eternal, needing no
more.

Each moment a portal, each breath a key,
Opening the stillness that sets me free. In
this meditative embrace, I return,
To the flame of awareness, forever to burn.

Meditation: Resting in Awareness

While Self-inquiry is the direct path, meditation is its companion. Meditation helps quiet the mind, creating space for the awareness of "**I AM**" to arise naturally. Unlike techniques that involve visualizations or affirmations, this meditation focuses on *being* rather than *doing*. It is meant for stabilizing awareness and abiding in the present moment. It helps us cultivate clarity, stillness, and non-attachment. Through regular meditation, we train ourselves to let go of distractions and connect with our inner peace.

Meditation, as part of Right Practice, is not about controlling the mind or forcing a state of calm. Instead, it's a gentle return to awareness, a way of observing the natural flow of thoughts, sensations, and emotions without attachment. Over time, meditation strengthens our ability to remain centered in any situation, helping us approach life from a place of inner stability and clarity.

Meditative abidance is a practice of returning to "**I AM**." By regularly meditating on the feeling of "**I AM**," we cultivate a deep, abiding awareness that becomes our foundation in every aspect of life. This presence is not tied to a particular thought or state; it is simply the awareness of "**I AM**."

Meditation Practice: Abiding in "I AM"

1. Sit comfortably in a quiet space.
2. Close your eyes and bring your attention to the sense of being—"**I AM**."
3. Don't try to define or analyze it. Simply rest in this awareness.
4. If thoughts arise, let them pass like clouds, gently returning to the sense of "**I AM**."

Over time, this practice deepens, allowing you to experience the stillness and peace that is always present.

Expanded Meditation Routine

For readers ready to deepen their meditation practice, here's an expanded routine that includes steps for both settling the mind and observing deeper layers of awareness:

1. **Begin with Breath Awareness:** Find a comfortable position, sitting upright but relaxed. Close your eyes, take a few deep breaths, and let go of any tension in the body. As you settle, bring gentle attention to your breath, noticing the natural rhythm of each inhale and exhale.
2. **Expand Awareness to the Body:** After a few minutes, expand your awareness to include the entire body. Feel the points of contact between your body and the floor or chair. Notice sensations—warmth, coolness, pressure, or even subtle tingling. Allow yourself to be fully present with these sensations, observing them as they naturally change and flow.
3. **Observing Thoughts as Clouds:** Now, shift your focus to observing thoughts. Rather than engaging with each thought or following it, simply let it arise and pass, like a cloud drifting across the sky. Remind yourself that thoughts are temporary and do not define you. Return to your breath if you become caught up in a thought.

4. **Resting in Awareness:** After spending time observing thoughts, let go of focusing on anything in particular. Rest in a state of open awareness, where you're simply observing without attachment to thoughts, breath, or sensations. This stage of meditation allows you to experience moments of pure being, where awareness rests in itself.
5. **Closing the Meditation:** Gently bring yourself back to breath awareness, then to body awareness, and slowly open your eyes. Take a few moments to stretch or move mindfully, carrying this sense of calm presence with you as you transition back to your daily activities.

Section 3

Silence and Stillness as Pathways to "I AM"

"Silence is the language of '**I AM**'."

"Stillness is the ground of being, where the illusions of the mind dissolve and the essence of '**I AM**' shines effortlessly. In the embrace of stillness, life's noise quiets, revealing the eternal peace that was never absent, only unnoticed."

"Silence is not the absence of sound; it is the presence of truth. It is peace, it is bliss, and it is the very nature of the Self. To realize this, simply be still—there is nothing the mind needs to do, no thought it needs to think. In stillness, the Self reveals itself effortlessly."

The Voice of Silence

In the stillness where no words reside,
The truth of being will not hide.
A quiet depth, a boundless sea,
The silence speaks, "I AM" to me.

No thought to follow, no sound to hear,
Just the essence, calm and clear.
The mind dissolves, its chatter stilled,
And peace within is gently filled.

Silence isn't empty; it's full of grace,
A timeless presence, a sacred space.
Not an escape, but life's true art,
To rest in the silence of the heart.

Through breath, through pause, through mindful care,
We touch the stillness always there.
In every moment, let it unfold,
The voice of silence, quiet and bold.

Silence is more than the absence of speech or sound; it's a state of inner stillness, where the mind quiets and we experience ourselves as is. It is the space in which truth reveals itself. It is the highest level of teaching – showing that words can point to the truth but cannot capture it.

In a world filled with noise and constant stimulation, cultivating silence is a profound way to reconnect with the peace within. Silence is one of the most powerful practices for realizing "**I AM**." In silence, we let go of the mind's endless activity and rest in the awareness that remains.

When we embrace silence, we step out of the mind's endless activity and settle into a space of calm. This practice helps us see that we are not our thoughts or emotions; we are the still and silent observing awareness behind them. By making room for silence in our lives, we allow ourselves to touch the depth of our being.

I encourage silence not as an escape from life, but as a way to connect with the essence of life itself. We spend so much time trying to fix things, to change people or control situations, as though we're directors of the universe. Silence teaches us that the only thing we need to 'fix' is our own knowing.

The Practice of Inner Silence

1. **Daily Quiet Time:** Set aside ten to fifteen minutes each day to sit in silence. Choose a comfortable place where you won't be disturbed and simply sit with your eyes closed. Let thoughts arise and pass without engaging with them, focusing instead on the silence that exists between thoughts. Focus on the feeling of "**I AM**," resting in the awareness that is always present. This silence reveals a depth of peace that is unaffected by external noise or thoughts.
2. **Breath Awareness:** Focus on your breath as a way to deepen into silence. Notice each inhale and exhale, letting the rhythm of your breath bring you to a place of stillness. This focus helps quiet the mind and allows you to experience a state of pure being.
3. **Mindful Listening:** Throughout the day, practice mindful listening. When others speak, give your full attention without planning a response. Listen not only to the words but also to the spaces between them. This helps cultivate an inner silence that remains present even during conversation.
4. **The Pause Practice:** Throughout the day, pause and ask, *"Am I aware?"* Let this question bring you back to the present moment.

Reflection on Silence

Take a few minutes after each session to reflect on how silence affected your awareness. Did you notice moments of clarity or calm? Were there any challenges in maintaining silence? As you practice, observe how silence brings greater peace and clarity into your life.

Section 4:

Practicing Non-Attachment with the Knowledge of "I AM"

"Freedom lies not in having, but in being."

"Renunciation is non-identification of the Self with the non-self. On the disappearance of ignorance the non-self ceases to exist. That is true renunciation."

The Art of Letting Go

The river flows, it does not cling,
To the rocks, the bends, or the songs it sings.
It moves with ease, through joy and strife,
A mirror of the flow of life.

Non-attachment is not to deny,
But to live each moment and let it fly.
Not holding too tight, nor pushing away,
Simply resting in the dance of the day.

"I AM" remains, unshaken, still,
Beyond the tides of want and will.

What I possess, what I release,
Cannot disturb this inner peace.

Let go of the fear, the grasp, the fight,
And walk in the freedom of the light.
The world will turn, as it always does,
But the Self is timeless, simply because.

So flow like the river, steady and true,
With nothing to gain and nothing to lose.
Non-attachment is the secret key,
To the boundless joy of being free.

What is Non-attachment?

Non-attachment is often misunderstood as detachment or indifference, but in truth, it's a state of being fully engaged in life without clinging to specific outcomes or identifying with external events. Non-attachment means experiencing everything fully and allowing it to pass naturally, without grasping or resistance. It's about embracing the flow of life without needing to control or possess it. When we are rooted in the awareness of "**I AM**," we realize that our happiness and peace don't depend on external conditions. This realization naturally leads to non-attachment.

Consider a river flowing effortlessly, adapting to its path without resisting obstacles. The river doesn't cling to any particular bend or try to avoid rocks—it simply flows. In the same way, non-attachment allows us to move through life with ease, adapting to changing circumstances without feeling bound by them.

A friend one day bought a new car. At first, he was overjoyed, polishing the car every day. But as time passed, the excitement faded, and the car became just another object. It's funny how much we attach to things that don't last. When we realize that peace comes from within, these attachments lose their hold on us.

The "Neti-Neti" Practice:
The Practice of "Not This, Not That"

"The ultimate truth is not found by adding more knowledge, but by removing everything that is false."

"At first, one must be guided to see that they are not merely the body, for identification with the body is deeply ingrained. However, the ultimate realization is not about rejecting the body but recognizing that one is both the body and all that exists–unlimited awareness itself. The key is to first discern between pure consciousness and the inert, impermanent body. This is true discrimination (*viveka*). Holding onto this understanding leads to liberation, where one abides as pure consciousness alone, free from limitation."

What is Neti-Neti?

Neti-Neti is a Sanskrit phrase that means **"Not this, not that."** It is a profound method of Self-inquiry and negation-based meditation used in the path of non-dualism philosophy to realize the true Self. The practice involves systematically negating everything that is not the real "I"— disentangling awareness from the body, thoughts, emotions, and external identities to uncover the pure, unchanging presence of "**I AM**."

Why is Neti-Neti Important?

Our suffering arises from misidentification—mistaking transient aspects of experience (body, mind, roles, thoughts) as the true Self. By using Neti-Neti, we eliminate what is impermanent, revealing the eternal awareness that remains.

This practice allows us to:

- Dissolve false identifications with thoughts, emotions, and perceptions.
- Move beyond the ego's limitations and recognize the boundless nature of awareness.
- Rest in the pure presence of "**I AM**" rather than being caught in mental fluctuations.

How to Practice Neti-Neti?

The practice of Neti-Neti can be done through structured Self-inquiry or meditative contemplation. Here's a step-by-step guide:

Step 1: Begin with Awareness of the Body

- Sit in silence, take a few deep breaths, and become aware of your body.
- Observe your physical form—your hands, face, posture, and sensations.
- Now, ask yourself "Am I this body?"
- If your body changes, ages, and eventually perishes, how can it be your true essence?
- Mentally affirm: **"Not this—Neti." "Not this—Neti."**
- Let go of identification with the body and move deeper.

Step 2: Observe Thoughts and Mind

- Turn your attention inward and observe the flow of thoughts in your mind.

- Notice that thoughts arise and pass—sometimes joyful, sometimes anxious, sometimes silent.
- Ask yourself "Am I these thoughts?"
- If thoughts constantly change and you remain aware of them, then who is the observer?
- Affirm: **"Not this—Neti." "Not this—Neti."**
- Let go of identification with thoughts and move deeper.

Step 3: Detach from Emotions and Sensations

- Notice emotions—joy, sadness, anger, peace—rising and falling like waves.
- Ask: "Am I these emotions?"
- Emotions are temporary experiences, but your awareness remains untouched.
- Affirm: **"Not this—Neti." "Not this—Neti."**
- Release attachment to emotions and move deeper.

Step 4: Question the Ego and Identity

- Reflect on the roles you play—parent, professional, friend, seeker.
- Ask: "Am I these identities?"
- If roles are situational and ever-changing, can they define your true Self?
- Affirm: **"Not this—Neti." "Not this—Neti."**
- Drop all identities and rest in presence.

Step 5: Beyond Perception—Rest in Pure Conscious Awareness

- By negating everything that is not you, what remains?
- The pure witnessing presence, silent and still.
- This awareness is not an object—it is what sees all objects come and go.
- No thoughts, no forms—just "**I AM.**"

At this point, there is nothing left to negate. You are left with pure awareness—boundless, unchanging, and free.

The Power of Neti-Neti: What Happens Through This Practice?

- You detach from false identities that cause suffering.
- You experience freedom from mental fluctuations.
- You shift from personal identity to pure conscious awareness.
- You realize your eternal nature beyond birth, death, and form.

By continually practicing Neti-Neti, awareness loses its attachment to limitations and rests in its natural, formless state. The mind becomes silent, ego dissolves, and the peace of "**I AM**" remains.

The Practice of Letting Go

One way to cultivate non-attachment is by observing areas in life where attachment creates tension. Start by identifying common sources of attachment, such as desires, fears, relationships, or material possessions. Notice how these attachments affect your peace of mind, leading to worry, anxiety, or disappointment when things don't go as expected.

Each day, practice letting go of one small attachment. For example:

- If you're attached to a specific outcome at work, remind yourself to focus on doing your best without obsessing over the results.
- If you find yourself worrying about a loved one, practice sending them love and compassion while releasing control over their choices.

Over time, this practice of letting go fosters a state of freedom, where you can appreciate life's experiences without being weighed down by expectations.

Reflection on Non-Attachment

Take a few moments to reflect on an area of your life where attachment has caused suffering. Ask yourself:

- *What am I clinging to in this situation?*
- *How would I feel if I released this attachment?*
- *Can I trust the flow of life, even if the outcome is uncertain?*

Write down your reflections and revisit them periodically. As you become more aware of attachments, you'll find it easier to let go, experiencing greater peace and flexibility.

Exercise in Non-Attachment

Letting Go of One Attachment: Identify one attachment in your life—something you believe you "need" for happiness. It could be a goal, a possession, or an expectation. Reflect on how "I AM" remains unchanged, whether or not you have this thing. Allow yourself to mentally release this attachment, experiencing the freedom that arises when you let go.

Section 5:

Right Action with the Understanding of "I AM"

The Grace of Right Action

In the stillness of "I AM," I see,
The path unfolds effortlessly.
No need for fear, no need for gain,
Each step I take, free from strain.

Right Action flows from a heart at peace,
Where ego's clamor begins to cease.
Not bound by outcomes, nor driven by will,
But guided by truth, steady and still.

Pause before the words take flight,
Ask if they serve the soul's true light.
In kindness and love, let actions grow,
A reflection of the Self we know.

Each deed a ripple, vast and wide,
Flowing with grace, where love resides.
No grasping, no force, just being clear,
Acting from the truth that's always near.

Right Action asks not for reward,
But finds fulfillment in the accord.
When the "I AM" guides, no task feels small,
For in each moment, we honor the All.

"Right action arises naturally when rooted in awareness of '**IAM**.'"

"Action is inevitable; no one can remain without acting. Life unfolds according to its own rhythm, regardless of personal will. Instead of resisting or trying to control it, allow the purpose of your existence to fulfill itself effortlessly. Surrender to the flow, knowing that you are not the doer but the ever-present awareness in which all action arises and subsides."

Actions performed with awareness, free from attachment to outcomes, align with the flow of life. When you act from the ego, your actions are often driven by fear, desire, or the need for validation. However, when you recognize that "**I AM**" is already whole and complete, actions become effortless expressions of truth and harmony.

A tree doesn't force itself to bear fruit; it happens naturally when the tree is rooted and nourished. Similarly, when you are grounded in the awareness of "**I AM**," your actions flow naturally, free of strain or conflict.

"Right action is action without the sense of personal doership."

"Karma will unfold and bear its fruits naturally. As long as you believe yourself to be the doer, you remain bound to the fruits of karma; The moment you release the illusion of being the doer, you transcend both karma and its effects."

The belief that "'I **AM**' the doer" creates attachment and suffering. When you see yourself as the witness of action, rather than its agent, you act with clarity and detachment. This does not mean passivity; it means acting from a place of freedom rather than compulsion.

Imagine flowing with a river instead of swimming against its current. Acting without a sense of doership is like flowing naturally with life, where effort becomes joyful and aligned with the larger whole.

Right Action, in the context of the Three-Fold Path, means acting from a place of inner clarity rather than ego-based desires or fears. When we are calm, centered and mindful, our actions naturally align with truth and compassion.

Right Action is about responding to life with awareness, whether we're making major decisions or interacting in daily relationships. It's an expression of our true nature, free from the pressures of attachment or fear.

Applying Right Action in Daily Life

Once you cultivate clarity and calm through the practices mentioned above, Right Action becomes an extension of this inner state. Here are ways to apply Right Action in everyday situations:

- **Pause Before Responding**: In challenging situations, take a moment to pause and observe your initial reaction. Ask yourself if this reaction aligns with peace, compassion, or ego-driven desires. By creating this pause, you open space for a mindful response.

- **Set Intentions for Actions**: Whether you're working, interacting with loved ones, or making decisions, start each activity with a clear, conscious intention. Setting an intention, such as "May my words bring kindness" or "May I approach this task with integrity," keeps actions aligned with your deeper values.
- **Practice Non-attachment in Action**: Right Action involves doing your best without clinging to specific outcomes. Focus on the quality of your actions rather than the results, trusting that life will unfold as it's meant to. This frees you from the stress of controlling every situation and allows you to act with a sense of freedom and peace.

Right Action naturally follows, arising from a mind that is clear, open, and compassionate. Through Right Action, we bring harmony into the world around us, contributing to a more peaceful and joyful life not only for ourselves but also for those we encounter.

Section 6

Surrender as a Natural Outcome

"Surrender is nothing more than to know one's true nature"

"Bhakti (devotion) and Self-inquiry are not two different paths; they lead to the same truth. The Self that the Advaitins (non-dualists) realize through inquiry is the very same God that the devotees surrender to in love. Whether through devotion or inquiry, both dissolve the illusion of separation and reveal the same ultimate Reality."

The Flow of Surrender

In the stillness of knowing, I cease to strive,
The need to control no longer alive.
Surrender arises, not born of defeat,
But a union with life, serene and complete.

The river flows, it knows its way,
Through rocks and bends, night and day.
No hand can force it, no will restrain,
Its journey is ease, untouched by pain.

To surrender is trust, a soft release,
An end to resistance, a path to peace.
Not passive, but present, alive, aware,
In the essence of "I AM," I'm fully there.

The grasping mind, the clinging hand,
Gives way to the flow, the open land.
In letting go, I find my part,
Life unfolds as art upon art.

So here I rest, in the truth I see,
That all I sought was already me.
Surrender is freedom, the ultimate goal,
The return to my essence, the infinite soul.

Surrender is the natural outcome of recognizing "**I AM**." When you see that awareness is whole and complete, you let go of the need to control or resist life. Surrender doesn't mean passivity; it means aligning with the flow of life, trusting that "**I AM**" is the essence of all that unfolds. Surrender is an act of unconditional trust, acknowledging that we don't need to control every aspect of life to be at peace. It's an acceptance of life as it is, grounded in the knowledge that "I AM" is always whole and complete.

Imagine trying to control the flow of a river. The more you resist, the more struggle and frustration you experience. But if you surrender to the river's flow, allowing it to carry you, you experience ease and freedom. Surrender is similar—it's a willingness to release resistance and allow life to carry you.

Daily Practice of Surrender

1. **Identify Areas of Resistance**: Begin by identifying areas in your life where you feel resistance, worry, or a need for control. This might be related to a relationship, career, or personal goals.
2. **Practice Letting Go**: For each area of resistance, take a moment to acknowledge your desire for control, and then consciously release it. You might say to yourself, "I surrender this situation to life." Let go of any attachment to specific outcomes and trust that things will unfold in the best possible way.
3. **Gratitude as Surrender**: Practice gratitude as a form of surrender. Each day, reflect on something you're grateful for, allowing gratitude to replace worry or control. By focusing on gratitude, you shift from resistance to acceptance.

Reflection on Surrender

Journal about your experiences with surrender. How does it feel to let go of control in specific areas? Are there areas where surrender is easier or more challenging? Use these reflections to deepen your practice, noticing how surrender brings peace and openness into your life.

Section Summary - Right Practice

Right Practice is the essential link between understanding and experiencing the truth of "**I AM**." It provides the means to stabilize awareness in daily life, allowing one to live with clarity, peace, and inner freedom. Each practice within this framework—Self-Inquiry, Meditative Abidance, Silence, Non-Attachment, and Surrender—serves a unique purpose but is deeply interconnected. Over time, these practices evolve into a seamless and unified experience, culminating in the ultimate states of silence and surrender.

Self-Inquiry is the foundation of Right Practice. The simple yet profound question, *"Who am I?"* peels away layers of false identification with the body, thoughts, roles, and emotions. It leads the practitioner inward, beyond the transient aspects of self, to the silent awareness of "**I AM**." Self-inquiry does not seek verbal answers; rather, it redirects attention from external identifications to the eternal presence that underlies all experience. This clarity provides the groundwork for other practices, as it exposes the illusions of the ego and creates space for deeper stillness.

Building on the insights of Self-inquiry, Meditative Abidance helps stabilize awareness in "**I AM**." Through meditation, the practitioner rests in pure being, observing thoughts, emotions, and sensations without attachment. Meditation fosters an inner stillness that allows the awareness of "**I AM**" to arise naturally. It is not about controlling the mind but about gently returning to the presence that is always there. As the mind quiets, meditation strengthens the foundation of inner peace, paving the way for silence to emerge.

Silence, in this context, is more than the absence of sound; it is the profound stillness in which truth reveals itself. In silence, the ego's chatter dissolves, and the practitioner directly experiences the unchanging awareness of "**I AM**." Silence arises naturally from Self-inquiry and meditative abidance, as these practices prepare the mind to rest in stillness. It deepens non-attachment by showing the impermanence of thoughts, emotions, and external experiences. Ultimately, silence becomes a sacred space where the practitioner abides in the peace and clarity of pure conscious awareness.

Non-attachment is another critical aspect of Right Practice. It is not about disengaging from life but about fully experiencing it without clinging to specific outcomes or identifying with external objects, roles, or desires. By understanding that happiness and peace come from within, non-attachment liberates the practitioner from the ego's grip. This state of freedom arises naturally through Self-inquiry, as the practitioner recognizes they are not their thoughts, roles, or possessions. Meditative abidance and silence further strengthen this detachment, making it easier to release control and trust life's flow. Non-attachment lays the groundwork for surrender, as it teaches the practitioner to let go and align with the present moment.

Surrender is the culmination of all practices within Right Practice. It is the act of fully trusting the flow of life and releasing all resistance and control. Surrender is not passive; it is a profound alignment with the truth of "**I AM**"—a recognition that awareness is whole and complete. As silence deepens and the attachments of the ego fall away, surrender arises naturally. It marks the end of spiritual striving, where the practitioner rests fully in the awareness of "**I AM**," experiencing life as an effortless flow of harmony and grace.

While these practices may initially seem distinct, they are deeply interconnected and mutually reinforcing. Self-inquiry uncovers the truth of "I AM," which meditative abidance stabilizes, silence deepens, non-attachment strengthens, and surrender fulfills. As the practitioner progresses, the boundaries between these practices blur, and they become a singular, unified experience. What begins as deliberate effort gradually dissolves into a natural state of being, where silence and surrender are no longer practices but the effortless expression of the realized Self.

In the culmination of Right Practice, silence becomes the natural resting place of awareness, and surrender becomes the effortless way of living in harmony with truth. At this stage, there is nothing left to seek or do, as the realization of "I **AM**" becomes the foundation of every experience. The practitioner lives from a place of peace, joy, and freedom, unburdened by the illusions of ego or the need for control.

"Right Practice is not about adding more, but about removing what is false. What remains is the simplicity of silence and the grace of surrender."

Through the integration of these practices, the timeless awareness of "**I AM**" shines through, revealing the true essence of the Self.

In the next chapter, we'll explore Right Experience, the culmination of Right Understanding and Right Practice, as we move toward living fully in alignment with our true nature.

This concludes Chapter 2: Right Practice. We've covered the following core ideas:

- ***Self-Inquiry:***
    - *Core practice of asking "Who am I?" to peel away false identities and discover the truth of* ***"I AM."***
    - *Encouraging exploring beyond roles, beliefs, and thoughts to recognize pure conscious awareness.*

- ***Meditative Abidance:***
  - *Stabilizing awareness in "**I AM**" through regular meditative abidance practices.*
  - *Focus on resting in pure conscious awareness, beyond thoughts and distractions.*
- ***Silence and Stillness:***
  - *Cultivating inner silence to experience the depth of "**I AM.**"*
  - *Silence is presented as a pathway to uncover truth and peace.*
- ***Non-Attachment:***
  - *Letting go of clinging to desires, fears and outcomes.*
  - *Living fully engaged in life without dependence on external conditions for happiness.*
- ***Right Action:***
  - *Action rooted in awareness free from sense of doership, free from ego-driven motives or attachment to results.*
  - *Responding to life with clarity and compassion, aligned with the truth of "**I AM.**"*
- ***Surrender:***
  - *Trusting the flow of life and releasing resistance to align with the natural unfolding of events.*
  - *Surrender is seen as the culmination of practice, arising naturally from recognizing the essence of "**I AM.**"*

Chapter 3

Right Experience
Being the Truth

The Ocean of Being

A raindrop falls from the endless sky,
Not knowing where, not asking why.
It dances through rivers, through valleys it streams,
Chasing a whisper it heard in its dreams.

Through twists and turns, through loss and gain,
It seeks an end to its fleeting pain.
It clings to form, to name, to past,
Yet every shape dissolves too fast.

But one day, weary, it meets the sea,
And in that moment, it comes to be.
No longer a drop, no longer alone,
It sees at last—it was always home.

So too, the seeker walks the land,
Holding questions in trembling hands.
Who am I, and what is real?
What truth can thought or senses reveal?

Through joys and sorrows, through nights and days,
Through mind's illusions, through ego's maze,
Until at last, the veil is thin,
And silence calls from deep within.

No self to seek, no goal to find,
No chains remain to bind the mind.
For "I AM" is the ocean wide,
Where waves may rise, but none divide.

Beyond all names, beyond all form,
Beyond the self that once was born,
Not two, not one, no here, no there,
Just boundless being—pure, aware.

The "I AM" fades, its task complete,
What's left is vastness, silent, sweet.
No witness now, no shape remains,
Just stillness, free from loss or gain.

No death to fear, no birth to claim,
No need for words, no need for name.
Just presence, shining, clear and true,
And all is That, and That is You.

Right Experience - Being the truth

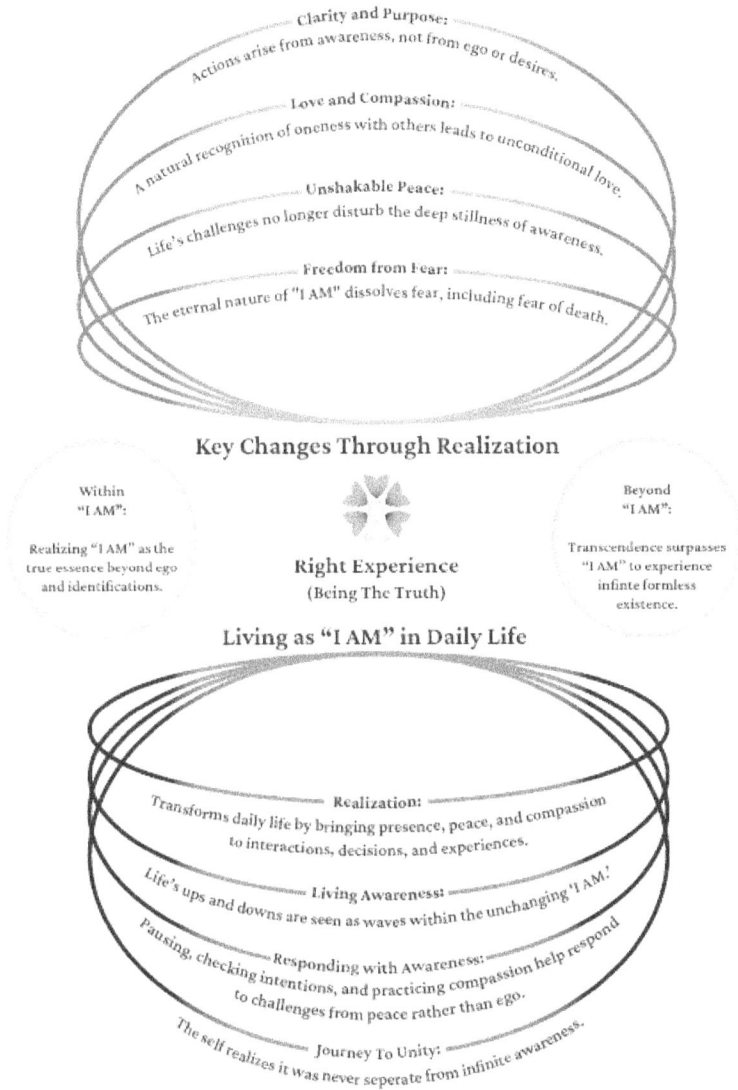

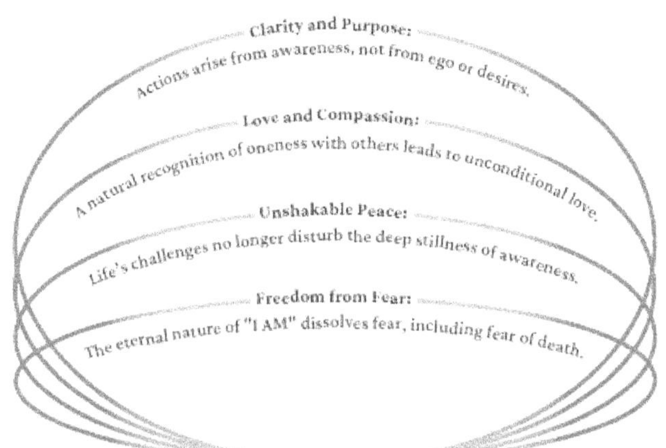

Clarity and Purpose:
Actions arise from awareness, not from ego or desires.
Love and Compassion:
A natural recognition of oneness with others leads to unconditional love.
Unshakable Peace:
Life's challenges no longer disturb the deep stillness of awareness.
Freedom from Fear:
The eternal nature of "I AM" dissolves fear, including fear of death.

Key Changes Through Realization

Within
"I AM":

Realizing "I AM" as the true essence beyond ego and identifications.

Right Experience
(Being The Truth)

Beyond
"I AM":

Transcendence surpasses "I AM" to experience infinte formless existence.

Living as "I AM" in Daily Life

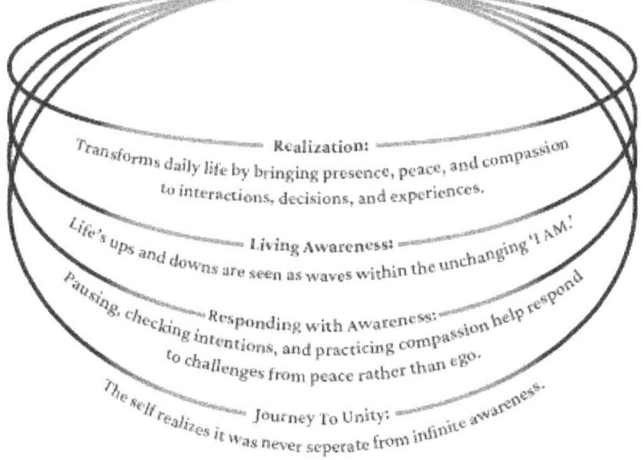

Realization:
Transforms daily life by bringing presence, peace, and compassion to interactions, decisions, and experiences.
Living Awareness:
Life's ups and downs are seen as waves within the unchanging 'I AM.'
Responding with Awareness:
Pausing, checking intentions, and practicing compassion help respond to challenges from peace rather than ego.
Journey To Unity:
The self realizes it was never seperate from infinite awareness.

Diagram 7: Key Concepts Covered in the Chapter

"The journey of seeking dissolves the moment you realize there was never anything separate to find. The Self is not a destination; it is the boundless being you have always been."

"Right experience is the stillness beyond all duality. When the illusion of separation fades, what remains is infinite awareness—whole, silent, and free."

Right Experience – Being the Truth

Realization & Transcendence of "I AM"

Right Experience is the culmination of the Three-Fold Path. It's the direct realization of our true nature—a state of being where peace, joy, and harmony flow naturally. Right Experience isn't something we can force or achieve through effort; rather, it arises when we fully embody Right Understanding and Right Practice. This experience is often described as Self-realization, enlightenment, or awakening. It's a state where we move beyond identification with the body and mind, resting in a timeless, boundless awareness that feels like coming home.

In Right Experience, we move beyond concepts and practices. Here, we experience "**I AM**" not as an idea, but as the living truth of our being. This chapter is about the flowering and culmination of our journey, where the illusion of separateness dissolves, and we find ourselves resting in the awareness that is beyond all identities, and then not even that.

Right Experience isn't something we can attain. It arises naturally when we let go of striving and settle into the simplicity of being. It is an experience of peace and joy that comes not from gaining something, but from realizing the essence that has always been present within us.

A single raindrop fell from the sky, landing on a high mountain. It began its journey down the slopes, gathering into a stream that wound through forests and valleys. The drop, now part of the flowing water, felt a deep longing to reunite with the ocean, the source it had heard whispers of in the rustle of leaves and the crash of distant waves.

As the stream grew into a mighty river, the drop remained restless, believing the ocean was a distant, unattainable destination. It endured obstacles—rocks, dry beds, and diversions—yet persisted, carried forward by an invisible pull.

One day, the river finally reached the vast ocean. As the drop entered its waters, it dissolved instantly, losing its individuality. But at that moment, it understood something profound: it had always been water. Whether as a drop, a stream, or a river, it had never been separate from the ocean. Its journey was not about becoming something new but realizing what it had always been.

The drop represents the individual self, or ego, which perceives itself as separate and longs for union with the infinite. The ocean is the Reality, the ultimate awareness of "**I AM**."

The drop's journey mirrors the spiritual path, filled with challenges, longing, and perseverance. But the realization at the end is that separation was always an illusion. The self has never been apart from Reality. It is, and always has been, one with the infinite.

Right Experience is this realization. You are not a separate individual trying to connect with something greater. You are already the infinite awareness you seek. Realization is not about becoming—it is about remembering.

Right Experience is about living from this place of inner clarity, allowing it to permeate thoughts, actions, and relationships. This chapter explores how realization transforms our understanding of life, removes the fear of death, brings freedom from fear, attachment, and the endless striving of the ego. It transforms your relationship with yourself, others, and the world, replacing division with unity and struggle with peace, bringing us into a profound connection with all beings.

In this state, you are no longer identified with the body or mind but live as the witness to all experiences. Joy and sorrow, success and failure, gain and loss—these are no longer opposites but are seen as waves on the ocean of awareness. The "**I AM**" remains unshaken, no matter how the waves rise and fall.

"You are the awareness in which all experiences arise and pass, but you yourself are not any of those experiences. You are the witness, not what is being witnessed. The moment you recognize this, you step beyond the illusions of the mind and rest in your true nature." To live as "**I AM**" is to abide in this truth, experiencing life without being bound by it.

In the end, even the "**I AM**," as profound as it is, must eventually be transcended. While it serves as the doorway, it is not the ultimate destination. The "**I AM**" arises spontaneously like an advertisement for pure awareness, but beyond this sense of being lies the Absolute Reality — silent, still, timeless, formless, thoughtless and infinite. This transcendence is not something to achieve but is eventually the natural outcome of realization. It is the recognition that you are not the body, the mind, or even the "**I AM**"—you are the source from which all appears to arise.

The Experience of Unity

With the disappearance of the ego, the illusion of separation dissolves completely. You begin to see that all forms, thoughts, and experiences arise from the same awareness. This experience of unity transforms how you relate to the world. Others are no longer "others"; they are expressions of the same consciousness.

In this state, love, compassion, and wisdom arise naturally. They are not qualities to cultivate but the essence of your being expressed freely.

Section 1:

Realization of "I AM": Within "I AM"

"To know '**I AM**' is to know peace."

"The '**I AM**' is the unshakable anchor of your being. Stay with it, and all illusions of mind and identity will dissolve, revealing the truth that has always been."

The Truth of "I AM"

In the stillness of being, I come to see,
The foundation of all is simply me.
Not the me of stories, desires, or name,
But the silent witness, eternally the same.

Like a wave chasing shores it cannot reach,
The ego grasps, striving to teach
That peace is found in things outside,
While the heart of truth has always lied.

"I AM" is the rope mistaken for snake,
The fear dissolves when we awake.
The wave is the ocean, the part is the whole,
In realizing this, I find my soul.

No longer bound by the ego's fight,
I rest in the peace of endless light.
Unshaken by storms, untouched by the flame,
The essence of being, ever the same.

In this awareness, I see it clear,
All that I sought was already here.
"I AM" is the anchor, the infinite grace,
The heart of existence, the timeless space.

Realization is the direct experience of "**I AM**" as the foundation of all existence. In this state, we see clearly that "**I AM**" is not a personal identity or a temporary state. It is the unchanging awareness that underlies every experience. This realization is not intellectual; it is a felt sense of being—an undeniable, direct knowing that transcends words.

When realization dawns, the layers of ego—the stories, identities, and attachments—begin to dissolve. We recognize that everything we've been seeking outside is already present within. Peace, love, and joy are not things we need to acquire; they are qualities of our true nature. In the silence of realization, we experience a deep inner peace, untouched by the fluctuations of the mind or the circumstances of life.

A sailor lost in a storm struggled to navigate the rough seas. Suddenly, a lighthouse appeared, guiding him safely to shore. The sailor realized the lighthouse had always been there; he just hadn't seen it before.

Realization is often described as the moment when we "see through" the illusions of the ego and recognize our true Self. This true Self is not a personality, a role, or a collection of beliefs. It's the silent, unchanging awareness that exists beyond thoughts, emotions, and identities.

This state has also been described as *"the Heart."* Here the Heart is not identified as a physical organ but the source of all existence—the Self. To abide in the Heart is to live from pure conscious awareness, free from the illusions of the mind.

Realization can happen suddenly, as an "aha" moment, or gradually, as a deepening awareness over time. Regardless of how it occurs, realization brings a profound sense of peace and clarity. We recognize that we are not separate individuals struggling in a world of division; we are one with the entire cosmos, part of an indivisible whole.

The Shift from Concept to Experience

Initially, the idea of "I **AM**" might feel like a concept—a thought you are contemplating. But with practice and inquiry, it transforms into a conscious living experience. This shift occurs when you stop trying to define "**I AM**" and instead rest in the direct awareness of it.

Realization is not a dramatic event or an intellectual achievement. It is a quiet, undeniable recognition of the awareness that you have always had. This realization dissolves the sense of separation, revealing the unity of all existence.

Imagine hearing a rustling sound in the dark and assuming it's a dangerous predator. Your heart races, and fear grips you. But when you turn on the light, you see it's just the wind moving the leaves. Instantly, your fear disappears. Similarly, when you shine the light of knowledge on the ego and recognize it as a false identification, the illusion dissolves, and the truth of "I **AM**" becomes self-evident.

Over time, realization deepens as we continue to release attachments and open to the spacious awareness within. This state of being brings a calm joy that isn't dependent on circumstances—it's simply the nature of the true Self.

How Realization Changes Your Life

- **Freedom from Fear:**

  Fear arises from the ego's attachment to outcomes, identities, and survival. ***When you realize that the "I AM" is eternal and untouched by the body or mind, fear begins to fade.***

- **Unshakable Peace**:

  Life's ups and downs no longer disturb the deep stillness of awareness. ***You meet joy and sorrow with the same equanimity, knowing that they arise within the unchanging "I AM."***

- **Love and Compassion**:

  Realization reveals that all beings share the same essence. ***This understanding naturally gives rise to unconditional love and compassion.***

- **Clarity and Purpose**:

  Actions no longer come from a place of lack or egoic desire but from the flow of awareness itself. ***Decisions are guided by clarity and inner alignment.***

Section 2:

Transcendence: Beyond "I AM"

"The ultimate freedom is the freedom from '**I AM**'."

"The '**I AM**' is the gateway to truth. Abide in it until even this sense dissolves, revealing the boundless Reality beyond."

"Existence and non-existence, unity and duality—these distinctions belong to the mind. In truth, nothing arises, nothing departs."

The Silence Beyond "I AM"

"I AM," the doorway, open and wide,
A truth revealed, where ego can't hide.
But beyond the door, no steps remain,
No "I" to carry, no self to sustain.

The sky dissolves, the clouds fade away,
No watcher remains to greet the day.
Not even the stillness claims a name,
Formless and boundless, all is the same.

No waves, no ocean, no ripple, no shore,
No seeker, no finding, no less, no more.
The "I AM" fades, its purpose complete,
What's left is the infinite, silent, replete.

Not two, not one, no boundary, no core,
A presence untouched by concept or lore.
This is the freedom, the ultimate grace,
Where even awareness finds no trace.

In life, it flows, in death, it remains,
Unmoved by joy, untouched by pain.
Beyond the knower, the known, and the seen,
Pure being shines, eternal, serene.

Realization is the doorway to transcendence. While realization is the direct experience of "**I AM**" as pure consciousness, transcendence involves moving beyond even this sense of "I" in "**I AM.**" In true transcendence, there is no longer a subject experiencing an object; there is only awareness (AM-ness) itself, beyond any notion of self, identity, or separation.

Transcendence occurs when you stop holding onto any sense of self, even the pure conscious awareness of being. What remains is the silent, infinite presence that cannot be described or grasped.

A bubble floated on the surface of a pond, marveling at its fragile form. It feared bursting, thinking it would cease to exist. But when the bubble popped, it realized it was never separate from the water.

Transcendence is the final letting go, the dissolving of even the subtlest sense of "I." In this state, awareness exists without a center, without any identity experiencing it. It is often described as "pure being" or "absolute awareness," a state where even the sense of beingness or consciousness of "**I AM**" becomes unnecessary.

Imagine the moment when a candle flame merges with the sunlight. As long as the candle is burning, it maintains its own identity, its own "**I AM**" as a separate light. But as it merges with the sunlight, it loses its separate identity and becomes part of the greater light. In the same way, transcendence is the dissolution or disappearance of "**I AM**" into just awareness.

Transcendence is the natural outcome of realization. It's the process of moving beyond identification with the body, mind, ego and even consciousness. In transcendence, we experience freedom from the limitations of any form of identity, opening to a vast and boundless awareness that encompasses all of existence.

This doesn't mean we abandon our human life or responsibilities. Instead, we live fully within the human experience, but without being bound by it. We engage with life from a place of unconditional surrender and non-attachment, fully present but free from the limiting beliefs and fears that once defined us.

The Experience of Transcendence through Realization

- **The Dissolution of Boundaries**:

  In transcendence, the distinction between self and other dissolves. You no longer perceive yourself as a point of awareness within a vast universe but as the boundless Reality in which all appearances arise.

- **Timelessness**:

  Time is revealed as a construct of the mind. In transcendence, you experience life as eternal, free from past, present and future.

- **Formlessness**:

  The sense of being an individual melts away. What remains is pure existence, beyond form or identity.

- **Freedom from Duality**:

  All opposites—good and bad, light and dark, self and other, dual and non-dual—are illusory and seen only as appearances arising from the same source. You rest in awareness where no distinctions exist.

How Transcendence Manifests in Daily Life

- **Effortless Presence:** *Actions flow naturally, without the interference of egoic desires or fears.*
- **Complete Acceptance:** *There is no resistance to life as it unfolds because there is no "me" to resist it.*
- **Silent Joy:** *A subtle, unshakable joy pervades all experiences, even in the midst of challenges.*

Analogies to Illustrate Realization and Transcendence

- **The Sky and the Clouds**: *Realization is like noticing the sky behind the clouds. Transcendence is recognizing that the sky and clouds are not separate—they both arise within the infinite.*
- **The Ocean and the Waves**: *Realization is like seeing yourself as the ocean rather than a wave. Transcendence is realizing there is no ocean or waves—only water.*
- **The Light and the Prism**: *Realization is recognizing yourself as the light. Transcendence is seeing that the light, prism, and colors are all one essence.*

Right Experience is not an end but a way of being. Realization brings you into the awareness of "**I AM**" and beyond. From this state, life is no longer a journey to achieve or become. It is a simple, effortless flow—a dance within the infinite. You are not in the world. The world is in you.

Section 3

Living as "I AM" in Daily Life

"When '**I AM**' is your anchor, all else flows."

"Ignore the ego and its movements; instead, focus on the light of awareness behind it. The ego is merely the thought 'I,' but the true 'I' is the ever-present Self."

Realization is not just a mystical experience to be enjoyed in meditation or retreat; it is meant to be lived. Living from the awareness of "**I AM**" transforms every aspect of our daily life. It brings a sense of inner peace that remains steady amidst life's ups and downs, a joy that is not dependent on external circumstances, and a love that naturally extends to all beings.

Living from the awareness of "**I AM**" means responding to each situation, person, and experience from a place of presence, compassion, and clarity. It means letting go of the need to control, judge, or protect the ego. Instead, we live with openness, trusting in the flow of life, knowing that "**I AM**" is always whole and complete.

This state of being isn't about withdrawing from the world; it's about engaging with life from a place of stability and openness. This awareness becomes your constant companion, helping you respond to situations with wisdom and compassion rather than reacting from ego or fear. Over time, this practice transforms your experience of life, allowing you to live with greater freedom, presence, and joy.

It's a state of profound peace and awareness that remains unshaken by life's fluctuations. When we live in the awareness of "**I AM**," we no longer need to seek validation or happiness from external sources; we recognize that the source of fulfillment is within us.

This state of being allows us to navigate life with greater ease and wisdom. Relationships improve as we no longer cling to others for our sense of self-worth. Challenges are met with equanimity, as we trust in the inner stability of our true Self.

Here are two events that happened in my life and how they differed in my response to each of them:

Before Realization: Navigating Grief Through Attachment

Before my transformation, my mother's passing struck me deeply, leaving me overwhelmed with anger, grief, confusion, and a profound sense of loss. I grappled with questions of why such pain had to exist, my mind seeking reasons and answers, caught in the web of attachment and identification with the roles of son and mother. My reactions were driven by the ego's need to cling to what was familiar and tangible, making her absence feel like an unbearable void. This emotional turmoil lingered, amplified by feelings of anger, guilt and helplessness, as I tried to reconcile my love for my mother with the impermanence of life. At that stage, I saw death as an event that fractured my sense of self and disrupted the harmony of my world.

After Realization: Witnessing Death Through Awareness

By the time I experienced the loss of my father, my transformation had brought a profound shift in my perspective. Anchored in the awareness of "**I AM**," I no longer saw death as an end or a rupture. Instead, I understood it as part of the natural flow of life, arising and dissolving within infinite awareness. My reaction to my father's passing was marked by a quiet acceptance and a deep sense of peace, free from resistance or attachment. I mourned, but my grief was not entangled in egoic identification. I saw my father not as a separate being but as an expression of the same eternal awareness that I experienced. This realization allowed me to honor my father's life with love and gratitude, while remaining centered in the unshakable stillness of my true nature.

Daily Reminder Practice:

Living in "I AM": *Throughout your day, pause and bring your attention to the feeling of "I AM." You can do this while waiting in line, eating, or even during a conversation. Let this awareness guide your responses, helping you act from a place of truth and compassion. Notice how this shifts your experience of daily life, making each moment an opportunity to live from your true Self.*

Integration with Daily Life

Right Experience is about bringing realization into every aspect of life. It's not enough to experience glimpses of peace and clarity during meditation; the goal is to carry this awareness into daily interactions, tasks, and challenges. Integration means living from the place of inner truth in all situations, allowing our realization to transform how we experience and respond to life.

Mindfulness in Action

Mindfulness in daily tasks is a powerful way to integrate realization. By bringing full presence to each activity, no matter how small, we break free from automatic patterns and experience life with fresh awareness. Here are a few simple ways to practice mindfulness in daily life:

1. **Mindful Eating:** Take a few moments before eating to appreciate your food. Notice the colors, textures, and aromas. As you eat, focus on each bite, experiencing the taste and texture fully. Eating mindfully not only enhances enjoyment but also helps you connect with gratitude for the nourishment provided.
2. **Mindful Walking:** Whether you're walking to your car, around your home, or in nature, practice walking slowly and

mindfully. Feel the sensation of each step, the movement of your body, and the connection to the ground. Allow yourself to be fully present in the act of walking, releasing any thoughts about your destination.

3. **Mindful Listening:** When in conversation, listen with your full attention. Set aside any urge to respond immediately or prepare a reply. Instead, simply listen, taking in the other person's words and emotions. This practice deepens connections and cultivates empathy.

Responding with Awareness

When challenging situations arise, it's easy to fall back into old patterns of reactivity. Right Experience invites us to respond from a place of inner peace rather than reacting from ego-driven emotions. Here are some ways to respond with awareness:

- **Pause Before Reacting:** When you feel triggered or upset, take a moment to pause. Breathe deeply and allow yourself a few seconds to settle before responding. This simple act of pausing can shift you from reaction to response.

- **Check Your Intention:** Before taking any action, ask yourself, "What is my true intention here?" Bringing awareness to your intention helps you act from a place of clarity and compassion rather than impulse or attachment.

- **Practice Compassion:** Realization brings an understanding that everyone is connected and that each person is on their own path. Practice viewing others with compassion, even when they challenge you. Recognize that their actions come from their own experiences and conditioning.

Section 4

Universal Love and Compassion as Expressions of "I AM"

"To love others is to recognize yourself in them."

"All that exists is nothing but my own Self. There is no separation, no duality—only the oneness of being. In this unity, there is no pain, no problems, only the completeness of love where everything is as it should be."

One of the most beautiful aspects of Right Experience is the natural arising of love and compassion. When we realize our true nature as "**I AM**," we no longer see ourselves as separate from others. We see that each person, each being, is a unique expression of the same awareness. This recognition brings forth a love that is not conditional or limited but universal.

This love is not an emotion; it's a state of being. It's the natural compassion that arises when we recognize that everyone is a part of the same consciousness. In this state, we feel a deep empathy for others, understanding that their joys and sufferings are also our own.

When we see ourselves as one with all of life, love and empathy become natural expressions of our true nature. We no longer need to force kindness or compassion; they flow effortlessly from an open heart. This universal love isn't limited to specific people or circumstances; it embraces all beings, recognizing their inherent worth and beauty.

I have a memory of a moment in a crowded marketplace. As I looked around, I felt a profound sense of love for everyone I saw—shopkeepers, customers, even people hurrying by with worried faces. In that moment, I felt the essence of "**I AM**" in each person, seeing beyond their personalities and roles.

Loving-kindness Meditation

This meditation is a practice that nurtures universal compassion. Here's a simple way to begin:

- **Begin with Yourself:** Sit quietly, close your eyes, and bring to mind a feeling of love and compassion. Imagine this warmth in your heart, and silently repeat, "May I be happy. May I be healthy. May I be safe. May I live with ease."
- **Extend to Loved Ones:** Next, bring to mind a loved one—someone who brings you joy. Imagine sending them the same wishes: "May you be happy. May you be healthy. May you be safe. May you live with ease."
- **Expand to All Beings:** Gradually expand your circle to include people you know, strangers, and even those you find challenging. Eventually, extend these wishes to all beings: "May all beings be happy. May all beings be healthy. May all beings be safe. May all beings live with ease."

This practice cultivates a sense of universal love and compassion, reminding you that all beings share in the same experiences of joy and suffering.

Reflection on Universal Love

Take a few minutes after each loving-kindness meditation to reflect on how it feels to send love and compassion to others. Notice any shifts in your heart or mind. Over time, this practice softens boundaries and deepens your sense of connection with the world.

Section 5

Beyond Birth and Death – The Timeless Nature of "I AM"

"In the awareness of '**I AM**,' there is no birth or death—only being."

"You were never born, and you will never die. The body and mind appear, change, and disappear, but the awareness that watches remains untouched."

One of the most profound realizations in Right Experience is the understanding that our true Self is beyond birth and death. While our body and mind are subject to change, decay, and eventual death, the awareness of "**I AM**" is timeless. It is the unchanging presence that exists beyond form, untouched by the cycle of birth and death.

Realizing the timeless nature of "**I AM**" dissolves the fear of death. When we see that awareness is not bound to the physical body, we understand that our true essence is eternal. This realization brings a peace that is not shaken by life's uncertainties, a freedom that allows us to live fully in the present moment.

Many spiritual traditions teach that true liberation is freedom from the cycle of birth and death. This doesn't mean we escape life; rather, we come to see that life is a continuous flow, with awareness as the unchanging witness. Realization brings the understanding that, even as our physical form changes and ultimately dissolves, the essence of who we are remains eternal.

Reflection on Impermanence: Contemplating Life's Cycles

To deepen your understanding of impermanence, spend a few moments each day observing the natural cycles around you. Notice the changing seasons, the growth and decay of plants, or the shifting colors and patterns of the sky. Reflect on how everything in the physical world is in a constant state of change. Let this observation bring you closer to the realization that, while forms are impermanent, the awareness witnessing these changes is timeless.

Contemplation of Timeless Awareness: Beyond Birth and Death

Spend a few minutes in quiet reflection, contemplating the nature of awareness. Ask yourself, "What is this awareness that remains the same in every experience?" Rest in this question without seeking an answer, allowing yourself to feel the presence of timeless awareness within. This contemplation helps dissolve the attachment to the physical self, bringing a sense of peace that is unaffected by the concept of birth or death.

Section Summary

Living from Right Experience

Right Experience transforms our understanding of life. It dissolves the illusion of separation, allowing us to experience life as an expression of universal love, compassion, and peace. By living from this state, we approach each moment as an opportunity to express our true nature, free from attachment and fear.

The journey of the Three-Fold Path culminates in Right Experience, yet it is also a beginning. It's an invitation to live with open awareness, to embrace life fully, and to find harmony in the present moment. As we deepen in realization, we come to know that peace, joy, and love are not distant goals—they are the essence of who we truly are.

This concludes Chapter 3: Right Experience. We've covered the following core ideas:

- ***Realization of "I AM":***

  Right Experience is the direct realization of "I AM" as the essence of our being. It involves transcending identification with the body and mind to rest in a timeless, boundless awareness.

- **Living Beyond the Ego:**

  Moves beyond concepts and practices into the state of pure awareness, dissolving the ego's illusions.

  The experience of unity replaces division, struggle, and fear with peace and harmony.

The Culmination of the Path:

Represents the flowering of Right Understanding and Right Practice into a lived reality.

Emphasizes that peace and joy are not external goals but inherent aspects of our true Self.

- ***Unity and Compassion:***

  Recognizes all forms and beings as expressions of the same awareness, fostering natural love and compassion.

  Relationships transform, becoming rooted in unity and empathy rather than roles and expectations.

- ***Timeless Awareness:***

  The fear of birth and death dissolves as one realizes that "I AM" is eternal and unchanging.

  Awareness transcends the ego's limitations, aligning life with the natural flow of existence.

- ***Practical Integration:***

  Encourages living from this awareness in everyday actions, bringing clarity, presence, and harmony into all aspects of life.

Journal for Reflection

Journal – A Place for Reflecting

The journey along the Three-Fold Path is one of continuous growth, and a journal can be a valuable tool for reflecting on and integrating the insights gained along the way. Journaling provides a space to document your thoughts, experiences, and challenges, helping you to stay connected with the process of self-discovery.

The Purpose of Journaling on the Path

A journal is more than a record of events; it's a mirror that reflects your inner journey. Writing down your reflections allows you to see patterns, track your progress, and uncover deeper insights. As you move through the Three-Fold Path, journaling can help you process realizations and anchor them in your daily life.

Each section in this book includes prompts and exercises designed to deepen your experience of Right Understanding, Right Practice, and Right Experience. Use these prompts as starting points for your journaling, allowing yourself to explore each question or exercise fully. Over time, you'll begin to notice the subtle transformations that occur as you integrate these teachings into your life.

Guided Prompts and Reflections

Use the following prompts to reflect on each phase of the Three-Fold Path. These questions are designed to help you go deeper into your understanding, practice, and experiences along the journey.

Right Understanding – Knowing the Truth

- Reflect on a time when you felt deeply connected to everything around you. How did this experience change your perception of yourself and others?
- What beliefs or assumptions do you hold about yourself? Which of these feel authentic, and which feel conditioned or limiting?
- Take a few minutes to observe your thoughts without judgment. What patterns or recurring themes do you notice?
- Reflect on the idea of non-duality. How does it feel to consider that all things are one and part of a single reality?
- Write about your relationship with the concept of "truth." What does truth mean to you? How do you know when you're experiencing it?

Prompts for Exploring "I AM" as Pure Consciousness

- Reflect on a moment when you felt deeply present. How did it feel to rest in that awareness? What did you notice about yourself and the world around you?
- What roles, labels, or identities do you currently hold? How do these identities shape your thoughts, feelings, or actions? Who are you without these roles?
- Write about a time when you felt a sense of connection with everything around you, as if you

were part of a larger whole. How did that experience change your understanding of yourself?

- What beliefs do you hold about yourself? Which of these feel like authentic expressions of your true nature, and which feel like learned patterns or conditioning?

Prompts for Observing the Mind and Thoughts

- Spend a few minutes observing your thoughts. Write down any recurring themes, worries, or desires. How does it feel to witness these thoughts without attaching to them?
- Reflect on how often your mind creates narratives or judgments about yourself and others. What would it feel like to let go of these stories, even briefly?
- Write about an experience where you felt liberated from the usual mind chatter—perhaps during meditation, a walk, or a quiet moment. How did this freedom impact you?

Right Practice – Remembering the Truth

- Identify an attachment in your life—a person, outcome, or material possession. Reflect on how this attachment impacts your sense of peace. How might you practice non-attachment in this area?
- After a session of Self-inquiry, write about any insights that came up. Did you notice any habitual identities or beliefs? How did it feel to let go of these, even momentarily?

- Describe your experience with silence and stillness. What arises when you allow the mind to quiet? How does silence affect your sense of self?
- Reflect on a time when you practiced surrender. How did it change your experience of the situation? What insights did surrender bring?
- After meditating, write about any changes in your mental state or emotional balance. How does regular meditation impact your interactions with others?

Practices

Right Practice involves grounding the awareness of **"I AM"** in daily life. These practices help stabilize this awareness, allowing it to become a constant presence. Try incorporating these exercises into your daily routine, using them as anchors to remind you of your true nature.

A gardener tended to her plants daily, watering them, removing weeds, and ensuring they had sunlight. Over time, her once-barren garden bloomed into a vibrant oasis.

Daily practices like Self-inquiry, meditative abidance, non-attachment, neti-neti, and moments of silence are the tools that nurture your awareness. Each small effort creates space for the awareness of **"I AM"** to flourish in your life.

Self-Inquiry

- **Daily Self-Inquiry:** Set aside a few moments each day to ask, "Who am I?" Observe what arises without attaching to any answer. Let go of each thought, and rest in the awareness that remains.

- **Questioning Beliefs:** When you notice a strong belief about yourself or the world, gently ask, "Is this truly who I am?" This practice helps dismantle limiting beliefs, allowing the deeper awareness of **"I AM"** to shine through.

Meditation on "I AM"

- **Abiding in "I AM":** In your meditation practice, focus on the feeling of **"I AM"** without adding any thoughts or labels. Allow this awareness to deepen, resting in the silence and stillness of pure being.

Silence and Stillness

- **Reflecting on the Practice of Silence and Stillness**

  1. What does silence feel like? Describe your experience of physical and mental silence. Is it empty, calming, or something else?
  2. What arises in silence? Reflect on the thoughts, emotions, or sensations that come up when you sit in silence. How do these change over time?
  3. How does silence impact your awareness of **"I AM"**? What happens to your sense of self in moments of stillness?
  4. How does noise affect you? Reflect on how external or internal noise (e.g., mental chatter) influences your sense of peace. How does silence help you detach from it?
  5. What does silence teach you about impermanence? Observe how moments of silence come and go, yet the

awareness behind them remains. How does this deepen your understanding of your true Self?

- **Practical Exercises for Silence**

  1. **Daily Quiet Time:** Set aside 10–15 minutes each day to sit in silence. Observe the stillness between thoughts, sounds, and breaths. Journal what arises in this space.
  2. **Listening to Silence:** Throughout your day, pause and listen for moments of natural silence (e.g., between sounds, breaths, or conversations). Notice how these moments anchor you in the present.
  3. **Silence in Conversations:** Practice mindful listening during interactions. Allow pauses in conversations and focus on the space between words. Reflect on how this deepens your connection with others.
  4. **Observing Noise Without Judgment:** When you're surrounded by noise, practice noticing it without labeling or reacting. How does this shift your experience?

Non-Attachment

- Letting Go of One Thing: Identify one small attachment each day—a worry, a desire, or an expectation—and mentally release it. Notice the sense of freedom that arises when you let go of needing a specific outcome.
- Reflecting on Impermanence: Spend time observing the impermanence of objects, people, or experiences in your life. By understanding that all forms are temporary, you'll find it easier to remain centered in the awareness of **"I AM,"** which is beyond change.

Practicing Neti-Neti

Use these prompts during or after your Neti-Neti meditation to deepen your Self-inquiry and reflection. They will help clarify insights, identify attachments, and guide you toward the realization of your true Self.

- Reflecting on Self-Inquiry and Negation

  1. What am I not? Reflect on an identity you frequently associate with (e.g., your profession, a role, or a personality trait). What remains when you mentally detach from this identity?
  2. What thoughts or beliefs feel most "me"? How does it feel to negate these thoughts as "Not this"? Who or what is observing these thoughts?
  3. Am I these emotions? Recall an intense emotion you experienced recently (e.g., anger, joy, sadness). Ask yourself, "Am I this emotion?" Who is aware of it?
  4. What arises when I negate my body? Spend a few moments reflecting on your physical sensations. How does it feel to affirm, "I am not this body"?
  5. Beyond the mind: Observe recurring patterns of thought or worries. Can you recognize that these thoughts are impermanent? Who is witnessing them?

Practical Exercises for Neti-Neti

1. **Daily Self-Inquiry:** Ask "Who am I?" during moments of stillness. Let each response (thought, label, emotion) dissolve as you affirm, "Not this, not that." Rest in the awareness that remains.

2. **Challenging Attachments:** When faced with a strong attachment (e.g., to a person or outcome), ask, "Is this truly me?" Practice mentally releasing the attachment.
3. **Observing Layers of Identity:** Journal about each layer of your perceived self (e.g., physical, mental, emotional). For each layer, affirm "Neti, Neti" and explore the awareness that lies beneath.

These journaling prompts allow you to reflect deeply on your inner journey and track the transformation that unfolds through the practice of Neti-Neti. Take your time with each prompt, revisiting them as your understanding and awareness deepen.

Right Experience – Being the Truth

- Describe a moment when you felt a glimpse of realization—a sense of knowing or seeing beyond ordinary perception. How did this experience feel?
- Reflect on an instance where you transcended ego-based reactions. How did it feel to respond from a place of awareness rather than conditioned patterns?
- Write about your experience of the **"I AM"** awareness. How does it feel to rest in this awareness, free from identities and roles?
- Describe a moment of universal love or compassion. What did it feel like to connect with others from a place of openness and understanding?
- Contemplate your understanding of life beyond birth and death. How does the concept of timeless awareness influence your perception of change and impermanence?

Reflection Prompts for Right Experience

As you deepen in Right Experience, use these prompts to reflect on your direct experiences of **"I AM"** and the insights that arise from living in this awareness.

Prompts for Realization

- Describe a moment when you felt a glimpse of **"I AM"** as pure conscious awareness, beyond thoughts and identities. How did it feel to experience this state directly?
- Write about a time when you felt a sense of connection with others that went beyond roles or personalities. How did this awareness of oneness impact your interactions?
- Reflect on any fears or resistances that arise around the idea of letting go of personal identity. What attachments or beliefs might be keeping you from fully experiencing **"I AM"**?
- How has your experience of **"I AM"** influenced your relationship with the concepts of birth and death? Has this awareness shifted your understanding of impermanence?

Prompts for Living as "I AM" in Daily Life

- Write about a situation where you responded from a place of presence and compassion rather than ego or reactivity. How did it feel to act from this awareness?
- Reflect on any moments when you felt naturally loving or compassionate toward others, even if they were

strangers. How does recognizing the **"I AM"** in others change your perception of them?

- Describe an experience where you felt grounded in **"I AM"** despite a challenging or stressful situation. What insights arose from handling the situation with this awareness?

Tracking Progress and Patterns

Regular journaling allows you to track your growth over time. As you review past entries, you may notice patterns or recurring themes that reveal your personal journey along the Three-Fold Path. This tracking can provide valuable insights into how your understanding and experiences evolve, showing you how your awareness deepens as you continue practicing.

- **Monthly Review:** At the end of each month, set aside time to review your journal entries. Notice any recurring themes, insights, or challenges. Reflect on your progress and observe how each phase of the path unfolds naturally as you continue practicing.
- **Identifying Patterns:** As you read your entries, pay attention to any patterns of attachment, resistance, or emotional reactions that arise. These patterns provide insight into areas where further growth or release may be beneficial.
- **Celebrating Milestones:** Recognize and celebrate the small shifts and realizations along the way. Each insight, no matter how subtle, is a sign of progress and a step closer to fully realizing the peace, joy, and harmony of your true nature.

Creative Expression

Journaling can also take the form of creative expression, allowing you to explore your inner journey through art, poetry, or storytelling. Creativity is a powerful way to connect with the truths you're uncovering and to express them in ways that resonate with your unique experience.

- **Art and Imagery:** Use drawings or collages to visually express concepts like non-duality, the **"I AM"** state, or the feeling of transcendence. These images can serve as reminders of your journey and evoke a deeper understanding beyond words.
- **Poetry and Prose:** Write poems, reflections, or short stories that capture your insights or emotional responses to the teachings. Poetry can be a particularly powerful way to express complex, subtle feelings that might be difficult to articulate otherwise.
- **Personal Narratives:** Document personal stories where you encounter challenges or experience moments of clarity. These stories not only serve as milestones on your path but also help you see how the teachings of the Three-Fold Path are gradually integrating into your life.

Gratitude Practice

Gratitude practice is a wonderful way to cultivate a positive mindset and reinforce a sense of peace and joy. Dedicate a section of your journal to gratitude and make it a habit to record things you're grateful for each day.

- Daily Gratitude Entries: Each day, write down three things you're grateful for. They can be simple things—a kind interaction, a moment of peace, or a beautiful scene in nature. Focusing on gratitude helps shift your perspective toward appreciation and openness.

- Gratitude for Challenges: Occasionally, reflect on challenges and difficult experiences and consider what lessons they have offered. This practice of "gratitude for challenges" fosters resilience and helps you approach life with an open heart, even in difficult moments.

Maintaining the Journey: Final Reflections

The journey along the Three-Fold Path is one of continual discoveries. It's a path that reveals new insights, challenges old beliefs, and invites us to live from the depth of our true being. The following reflections can serve as reminders as you continue your journey:

1. **Be Patient with Yourself:** Realization is a process, not a race. Each insight, no matter how small, is a step closer to experiencing **"IAM"** in its fullness.

2. **Stay Curious:** Approach each moment with openness and curiosity. Life itself becomes your teacher, revealing the essence of **"IAM"** in both the ordinary and extraordinary.

3. **Embrace Challenges as Opportunities:** Challenges are invitations to deepen your awareness. When difficulties arise, see them as chances to anchor yourself in the presence of **"I AM."**

4. **Celebrate Moments of Awareness:** Recognize and appreciate the moments when you experience peace, love, or connection. Each moment of awareness strengthens your connection to your true Self.

5. **Trust the Process:** The journey may not always be smooth, but each step brings you closer to the realization that peace, joy, and harmony are not distant goals but qualities of your own being.

A traveler kept a journal, recording her thoughts, experiences, and realizations as she explored the world. Years later, when she reread her entries, she discovered a profound truth: the journey was not about the places she visited but the self she discovered along the way.

Journaling and reflection are ways to deepen your connection with the Three-Fold Path. They help you recognize patterns, celebrate progress, and integrate the realization of **"I AM"** into your daily life.

Embracing the Three-Fold Path

Conclusion: Embracing the Three-Fold Path

As we reach the end of the book, it's important to remember that the journey doesn't end here; it's the beginning. Realization is not an escape from life, but a way to live more fully, more openly, and with a heart rooted in love and compassion. Each step—Right Understanding, Right Practice, and Right Experience—brings us closer to the realization that peace, joy, and harmony are not things we find outside, but qualities of our own being.

The Three-Fold Path is an invitation to live from a place of profound awareness, simplicity, and love. Through Right Understanding, we recognize the truth of our oneness. Through Right Practice, we cultivate habits that ground us in the present moment. And through Right Experience, we realize our true nature as boundless, timeless awareness.

Living from the awareness of **"I AM"** allows us to face life's challenges with grace, to connect with others in genuine love, and to see beauty in ordinary moments. This is the essence of the Three-Fold Path: not to become something new, but to uncover who we have always been.

This path is not about adding more to our lives but about letting go of what isn't essential. It's about shedding the illusions, attachments, and fears that obscure our natural state of peace, joy, and harmony. As you continue on this journey, remember that each step—no matter how small—is a step toward coming home to yourself.

A child played in a garden filled with toys and games. One day, he grew tired and sat under a tree. There, he felt joy and peace unlike anything the toys had given him. He realized he didn't need them to be happy; simply being was enough.

The Three-Fold Path leads you back to this childlike simplicity. It offers a lifetime of growth, discovery, and transformation. There will be moments of challenge and moments of grace, but each experience, taken with awareness, becomes a teacher along the way. Trust in the process, be patient with yourself, and know that what you seek is already within you, waiting to be uncovered.

May this book serve as a companion on your journey, guiding you back to the simple, timeless truth of who you truly are.

The Eternal Song of Self

The Eternal Song of Self

Within the silence of the eternal, I dwell,
Neither form nor name do I compel.
How does one bow to what cannot be seen,
The unborn essence, serene and supreme?

All words arise and fade in me,
I am the root of all that's free.
Beyond knowing, beyond not-knowing,
A formless tide forever flowing.

I call to myself, a voice so deep,
Through life's illusions, I slowly seep.
Grace floods my being, bliss overflows,
The light of myself is all that shows.

The "I AM" calls, a subtle snare,
Creating worlds, a dream we share.
Yet I see its fleeting guise,
Its illusions perish when I rise.

The knower, knowing, and known dissolve,
A trinity of questions I resolve.
I am the space where all rest ceases,
A wholeness of infinite, boundless pieces.

To myself, I turn, again and again,
Discarding the false, the fleeting pain.

For I am the truth, eternal and bright,
The witness of darkness, the source of light.

I ask myself, "What can perish here?"
The answer whispers, soft and clear:
"I am ever, unchanging, one,
The silent truth when all is done."

The "I AM" fades, its play undone,
Its shadows vanish in the sun.
The world dissolves, yet I remain,
The still observer beyond the plane.

No form defines me, no name can bind,
In formless truth, myself I find.
I rise beyond, I merge, I blend,
I am the beginning, I am the end.

Beyond the body, beyond the thought,
Freedom from all that time has wrought.
I see myself as the only key,
To unlock the truth, to simply be.

Oh Self of selves, I bow to thee,
For showing the path to eternity.
No birth, no death, no space, no time,
The stillness rings a soundless chime.

I tell myself, "Let go, be free,
What was, and is, is only me."
The voice grows quiet, words disappear,
In silent knowing, all is clear.

I am the sky, the earth, the flame,
The water, the wind, the endless name.

Yet untouched by these, I simply stand,
The one eternal, the vast, the grand.

No more "I AM," no separation,
No cause, no birth, no creation.
I see myself in all that seems,
The unity beneath life's dreams.

Thus, I merge, I end the strife,
I am the stillness, the formless life.
No duality, no fleeting disguise,
I am the truth where illusion dies.

This is my song, my eternal plea,
A call from myself to simply be.
To those who listen, to those who see,
The Self is the path, the Self is free.

Final Words From Sri Ashish

Final Words from Sri Ashish

"The only purpose of life is to know who you truly are."

"Realizing your true Self is the highest service to the world. When you awaken to your own nature, your very presence becomes a light that uplifts all."

There is no identification here with being a guru, sadhu, yogi, swami, or any other role the world may project. Labels belong to the mind, which seeks to define the indefinable. Once the imagined self dissolves, there is no one left to carry a name or role. The tendency to place personalities on pedestals leads to illusion and eventual disappointment—because that which is Real has no personality, no agenda, no need for recognition.

What arose once as a seeker was simply the movement of Consciousness seeking clarity through the experience of pain and suffering. That impulse gave rise to inquiry—not for the sake of becoming someone, but for the dissolving of all mistaken identities. There was a deep movement to understand, to uncover what is, and in that process, it became clear: there is nothing to become, only illusions to shed.

What is shared here is not teaching from a person, but the natural echo of understanding that remains when confusion ends. This path—what appears as the Three-Fold Path—is not a path to gain anything. It is gentle undoing, a return to what never left. If these words offer clarity or serve as a mirror to reflect the Truth already present within you, they have fulfilled their function.

Wisdom is not owned. The deepest insights expressed here have come through exposure to great beings, through contemplation, silence, and the vanishing of the false. They arise spontaneously, not from effort, but from stillness. They belong to no one—and thus, they are free.

Truth is **ever-silent, ever-still, ever-free**. To realize it is to see that suffering was a dream born of misidentification. When the veil lifts, there is no one left to suffer, only peace without center or boundary.

There are two great obstacles in this so-called journey: never beginning it and beginning without completing it. But in truth, there is no journey—only a waking from the sleep of separation. What seems like a path is a return to the **"I AM,"** and even that must dissolve, leaving only formless being.

No one awakens you. The light within reveals itself when the mind grows quiet. This book is not a doctrine, not a belief system. It is a mirror, pointing back to the One who has never changed. That One is what you are.

"You are already free, untouched by action, ever-luminous, and pure. Bondage exists only as long as you attempt to control the mind, mistaking stillness for something to be achieved."

"You are beyond all limitations—formless, changeless, and unmoving. The pure awareness that you are is without attachment, beyond all conditions and disturbances."

"There is nothing binding you. What is there for the limitless Self to renounce? Let go of the illusion of effort, allow the mind-body complex to rest, and abide in the peace that has always been yours."

If this is truly understood—not just intellectually, but with deep conviction—it has the power to dissolve all perceived bondage.

The words shared here are not teachings from a teacher but expressions from Silence, offered to the Silence within you. May they draw you inward to the unshakable stillness that has never been born and will never die.

That is the Self. That is the Truth. And That is You.

With Love and Blessings Always!

Some Questions You May Have

Frequently Asked Questions on the Three-Fold Path

1. **Who is Sri Ashish, and how is he related to the Three-Fold Path?**
   Sri Ashish is a spiritual teacher known for his teachings on Advaita Bhakti (non-dual devotion – Oneness of everything and Oneness in everything). He developed the Three-Fold Path to guide seekers toward Self-realization and inner harmony.

2. **What is the Three-Fold Path?**
   The Three-Fold Path is a spiritual framework comprising Right Understanding, Right Practice, and Right Experience. It offers a practical approach to rediscovering inner peace, joy, and harmony by aligning with the essence of **"I AM."**

3. **What are the main principles of the Three-Fold Path?**
   Right Understanding: Recognizing the true nature of reality and the essence of **"I AM."**
   Right Practice: Anchoring awareness in daily life through methods like Self-inquiry, meditative abidance, silence, and non-attachment.
   Right Experience: Realizing and living the truth of **"I AM"** in every aspect of life.

4. **What is the essence of "I AM" and why is it important?**
   "I AM" is the fundamental awareness present in all beings. It transcends identities, roles, and concepts, anchoring individuals in a state of pure consciousness. This essence is the silent observer of thoughts and emotions, unchanging and eternal.

"I AM" connects us to our timeless and complete nature, dissolving illusions of separation or inadequacy. Recognizing it brings profound peace, joy, and harmony, allowing us to live authentically from a place of inner stability.

5. **How does Right Understanding help in spiritual growth?**
   Right Understanding clears the illusions created by the mind, revealing the oneness of all life. It helps you see beyond the ego, uncovering the true essence of peace and joy within.

6. **What does non-dual reality mean?**
   Non-dual reality refers to the understanding that all existence is one undivided awareness. The apparent separations we perceive are illusions created by ego and mind. Beneath these layers lies the one essence of all things.

7. **What creates the illusion of separation?**
   The ego, through identification with thoughts, roles, and desires, creates a false sense of individuality and division from the whole.

8. **What is the mind and ego's role in our experience? How are they different from each other?**
   The mind (an aggregate of thoughts) serves as the instrument of perception, thought, and interpretation. It processes sensory input, organizes experiences, and forms memories. The mind is an essential tool for functioning in the world, enabling us to analyze, reflect, and respond to our surroundings.

   However, the mind is not our true essence. It is a temporary and fluctuating entity that arises within Consciousness. The mind is often restless, moving from one thought to another, leading to mental agitation. When not understood properly, it can reinforce illusions of separateness and suffering.

The ego (*Ahamkara*) is the false sense of individual identity. It is the "I-thought" that misidentifies itself as a separate being, distinct from the whole. While the mind functions as a tool, the ego creates the illusion of doership and attachment, leading to suffering.

The ego plays a role in:

- **Self-Identification** – It attaches to thoughts, roles, and personal narratives, believing them to be the "Self."
- **Separation and Duality** – The ego perceives distinctions between "me" and "others," reinforcing a sense of division.
- **Attachment and Desire** – It clings to identities, possessions, and external achievements, fearing their loss.
- **Suffering and Resistance** – The ego resists change, seeks validation, and reacts emotionally to perceived threats.

The ego operates through the mind. It arises due to ignorance (*Avidya*)—mistaking thoughts and roles for one's true nature. When identified with, the ego leads to suffering, as it is constantly seeking validation and avoiding impermanence.

Key Differences Between Mind and Ego

Aspect	Mind	Ego
Definition	Instrument of thought, perception, and cognition.	The false sense of identity that claims ownership over thoughts and actions.
Function	Processes information, enables reasoning, and organizes experiences.	Creates the illusion of individuality, attachment, and separation.
Connection to Awareness	Can be observed and used without identification.	Obscures awareness by creating a false sense of self.
Effect on Experience	A neutral tool that can be used for wisdom or confusion.	Causes suffering when mistaken as one's true nature.
State in Self-Realization	Becomes quiet, still, and functional without personal identification.	Dissolves as one recognizes the Truth of "**I AM**."

9. **How can we differentiate between ego and awareness?**
   Ego is attached to thoughts, emotions, and outcomes, whereas awareness observes these without clinging or aversion. Awareness remains unbound, unshaken and universal.

10. **What is the relationship between karma, free will, and destiny in the Three-Fold Path?**
    These concepts are seen as tools for learning and growth within the illusion of individuality. Awareness of **"I AM"** transcends karma, revealing a state of freedom from the cycles of cause and effect.

11. **How does Self-realization provide freedom from the cycle of birth-death-rebirth and free us from the fear of death and loss?**
    Birth and death of the body are appearances within Consciousness, not ultimate realities. The fundamental

misunderstanding is the identification with the body and mind rather than with underlying unchanging awareness. This false identification leads to fear—fear of death, fear of loss, and fear of the unknown.

In Truth, what we call "birth" is simply the appearance of **"I AM"** or Consciousness, and "death" is its disappearance. Neither touches the eternal Self, which remains unchanged beyond these transitions.

The Cycle of Birth, Death, and Rebirth

The concept of rebirth arises due to ignorance (Avidya) and attachment to the ego. When consciousness mistakenly identifies with the body (the destructible instrument), it imbibes an apprehension of its own destructibility and adopts the illusion of limitation and mortality. This false identification binds it to the cycle of karma, leading to endless desires, fears, and actions that sustain the illusion of rebirth. Liberation comes when one sees clearly that consciousness was never the body, never bound, and never subject to change.

Recognizing Unchanging Awareness breaks this cycle because:

- It reveals that we were never truly born as an individual self. The ego is merely a temporary illusion within consciousness.
- It dissolves the sense of personal doership. Without an ego to claim ownership over actions, karma loses its binding force.
- It brings freedom from desires and fears, which perpetuate reincarnation. When one no longer seeks fulfillment in external existence, there is no compulsion for rebirth.

By abiding in pure conscious awareness, rebirth becomes unnecessary because the illusion of individuality dissolves.

The fear of death arises because the ego clings to identity, possessions, relationships, and experiences. It perceives itself as a separate entity that can be extinguished. However, when we realize **"I AM,"** the fear of death vanishes because:

- The true Self is beyond time. It was never born and will never die.
- Death is merely a transition, not an end. Just as dreams appear and dissolve each night, life itself is a temporary projection within consciousness.
- Loss is an illusion. Awareness is ever-present and contains all experiences. Nothing real is ever lost, only expressed through manifestations.

A wave may fear dissolving into the ocean, believing it will cease to exist. But upon merging, it realizes it was always the ocean—never separate, never in danger. Similarly, when we recognize and realize the Unchanging Awareness, we understand that death is not an end but a return to what we have always been.

12. **What are the practices involved in Right Practice?**
Right Practice involves:

    - **Self-Inquiry:** Asking "Who am I?" to peel away false identities and connect with the essence of **"I AM."**
    - **Meditative Abidance:** Resting in pure conscious awareness to stabilize the mind.
    - **Silence and Stillness:** Cultivating inner peace by quieting the mind.

- **Non-Attachment:** Letting go of clinging to actions, outcomes or possessions.
- **Surrender:** Trusting the flow of life and aligning with the essence of **"I AM."**

13. **What is the purpose of Right Practice?**
    Right Practice aims to stabilize the realization of **"I AM,"** integrating this awareness into daily life through meditative abidance, silence, non-attachment and surrender.

14. **What is Self-inquiry?**
    Self-inquiry is the practice of asking the profound question - "Who am I?" This introspection peels away false identifications, revealing the pure conscious awareness of **"I AM"** as the ultimate truth.

15. **What is the role of meditative abidance in the Three-Fold Path?**
    Meditative abidance is a core practice that helps stabilize awareness in the present moment. By observing thoughts without attachment, it nurtures a connection to the peaceful essence of **"IAM."**

16. **How can silence and stillness aid in realizing "I AM"?**
    Silence allows the mind to quiet down, creating space for the essence of **"I AM"** to be experienced directly. It helps dissolve mental noise, revealing the unchanging awareness that underlies all experiences.

17. **How does the non-attachment enhance peace and freedom?**
    Non-attachment frees you from the need to control or cling to outcomes. By realizing that peace comes from within,

it becomes easier to navigate life with a sense of ease and adaptability. It fosters freedom and equanimity.

18. **How can non-attachment improve relationships?**
By releasing expectations and projections, non-attachment allows relationships to flourish authentically, rooted in compassion and understanding.

19. **What is the significance of surrender?**
Surrender is the act of trusting the natural flow of life, letting go of resistance and the illusion of control. It aligns us with our deeper essence of peace.

20. **What is right action?**
Right action refers to actions arising from awareness, free from ego-driven motives. Such actions are naturally aligned with harmony and truth.

21. **How does Right Experience differ from the other two principles?**
Right Experience is the culmination of Right Understanding and Right Practice. It involves living fully from the awareness of **"I AM,"** where every action and perception aligns with the truth of one's essence.

22. **How can I start incorporating the Three-Fold Path into my life?**
Begin with the practices of self-inquiry, meditative abidance, and moments of silence. Reflect on the nature of **"I AM"** and gradually integrate the principles of non-attachment and surrender into daily actions.

23. **How can we recognize "I AM" in everyday life?**
By cultivating presence, embracing silence, and observing thoughts without judgment, we become attuned to the

stillness of **"I AM,"** realizing it as the awareness behind all experiences.

24. **What does abiding in "I AM" mean?**
Abiding in **"I AM"** involves remaining centered in pure conscious awareness, regardless of external events, cultivating a life of inner peace and harmony.

25. **How does the Three-Fold Path help with fear?**
The path anchors us in **"I AM,"** the unchanging awareness that exists beyond the transient fears of the mind, offering a sense of security and freedom.

26. **How does the Three-Fold Path help with overthinking?**
By observing thoughts as transient and returning to the stillness of **"I AM,"** we reduce mental chatter and cultivate a sense of calm.

27. **How does the Three-Fold Path affect decision-making?**
Decisions become guided by clarity and alignment with inner truth rather than external pressures or reactive emotions.

28. **Can the Three-Fold Path help with daily challenges like stress or anxiety?**
Yes, the practices of the Three-Fold Path, such as Self-inquiry, non-attachment, and meditative abidance, help reduce stress and anxiety by anchoring you in the present moment and detaching from the mind's fluctuations. The path grounds us in the stability of **"I AM,"** dissolving stress rooted in over-identification with transient thoughts and external circumstances. Realizing **"I AM"** as unchanging awareness dissolves the fears and uncertainties rooted in ego, fostering a profound sense of peace.

29. **How does the Three-Fold Path transform relationships?**
The path fosters compassion and a sense of oneness, enabling us to interact with others from a place of authenticity and unconditional love.

30. **What is the role of compassion in this journey?**
Compassion arises naturally when we see all beings as expressions of the same undivided awareness, nurturing love and kindness.

31. **How can we maintain awareness during challenges?**
By observing emotions and responding from calm awareness rather than reacting impulsively, we maintain balance and presence.

32. **What is the role of persistence and patience in the Three-Fold Path?**
Persistent and patient perseverance supports the gradual unfolding of realization, helping us remain consistent and open as deeper insights arise.

33. **How can we let go of attachments?**
By recognizing the completeness of **"I AM"** and observing desires without attachment, we naturally release clinging.

34. **How does the Three-Fold Path redefine success?**
Success is seen as inner fulfillment and alignment with truth rather than external achievements or possessions.

35. **How does the Three-Fold Path affect creativity?**
The stillness of **"I AM"** allows creativity to flow effortlessly, unburdened by the mind's constraints or fears.

36. **What is the significance of gratitude?**
Gratitude shifts focus from lack to abundance, aligning us with the wholeness of our true nature and fostering joy.

37. **How does the Three-Fold path affect our sense of purpose?**
Purpose becomes aligned with authenticity and inner peace, driven by compassion and clarity rather than external validation.

38. **What is the role of observation in the Three-Fold Path?**
Observation cultivates mindfulness, enabling us to witness thoughts and emotions without becoming entangled in them, fostering inner clarity.

39. **Is the Three-Fold Path suitable for people of all beliefs?**
Yes, the Three-Fold Path is not tied to any specific religion or doctrine. It is a universal framework that guides seekers of all backgrounds toward inner harmony and Self-realization.

40. **What is the ultimate goal of the Three-Fold Path?**
The ultimate goal is to realize and live from the awareness of **"I AM,"** transcending the ego's illusions to experience genuine freedom and live a life of unchanging peace, joy, and harmony through unwavering connection to the Truth.

Appendices

Appendix 1

Suggested Reading and Resources

For those interested in exploring these teachings further, here are some recommended resources that complement the Three-Fold Path:

- **Books on Non-Duality and Spirituality**
    - I AM Ashish to "I AM" – by Dr. Anil Joshi
    - WHO AM I? The Teachings of Ramana Maharshi
    - The Nisargadatta Gita – by Pradeep Apte
    - Be As You Are: The Teachings of Ramana Maharshi edited by David Godman
    - "I Am That" by Sri Nisargadatta Maharaj
    - Tilopa's Wisdom by Khenchen Thrangu

- **For Advanced Readers:**
    - The Ribhu Gita/ Sri Siva Rahasyam – ISBN:978-81-8288-088-7 (Published by V.S. Ramanan, President Sri Ramanasramam – www.sriramanamaharshi.org)
    - Ashtavakra Gita (Archival Special Edition - Ramanasramam – www.sriramanamaharshi.org)
    - Avadhuta Gita – Translated by Swami Chetanananda
    - God Talks with Arjuna – The Bhagavad Gita by

Paramhansa Yogananda

- **Online Communities and Resources**
  www.ndpfoundation.com
  https://www.youtube.com/@OfficialNdpfoundation
  https://medium.com/@ndpfoundation

These resources provide additional insights, practices, and community support to help you deepen your understanding, practice and experience along the Three-Fold Path.

Appendix 2

Page Locations of the Figures

Glossary of Key Terms

Glossary of Key Terms

Advaita – A Sanskrit word meaning "not two." It refers to the non-dual reality — the understanding that there is no separation between the self and the Absolute. All is One. (pp. 9, 11, 158)

Awareness – The pure, observing presence that is prior to thoughts, emotions, and body. It is not something you do but what you are. (pp. 19, 21, 40, 46, 50, 53, 56–57, 58–59, 60–62, 64–66, 69–70, 75, 77, 79, 82–83, 85–86, 89, 91, 101–102, 113, 122, 127–129, 143, 161, 164, 167)

Bhakti – Devotion. In Sri Ashish's teachings, it refers to *Advaita Bhakti* — devotion to the Oneness in and as all things, beyond form or person-hood. (pp. 11, 96, 158)

Consciousness – The dynamic, aware principle that enables perception and experience. It is the first expression of the Self or Reality in form. (pp. 7, 19, 21–22, 24, 27, 36, 41, 46, 53, 57, 61, 69)

Destiny – The sequence of life events that unfold according to past actions (karma). Sri Ashish teaches that destiny operates only when we are identified with the ego. (pp. 7, 46, 62, 65, 68, 70, 161)

Doership – The sense that "I am the one doing," which arises from egoic identification. Freedom comes through releasing this illusion. (pp. 66, 68, 94-95, 102, 160, 162)

Ego – The false sense of individual identity constructed through thought, memory, conditioning, and personal narrative. It obscures the truth of one's real nature. (pp. 17, 19, 22–23, 27–28, 40, 46, 53, 62, 65–67, 73, 78, 90, 93, 102, 105, 112, 116, 128–129, 159, 161)

I AM – The primal sense of being or presence, prior to all labels or identities. It is the doorway to the Self but is ultimately transcended. (pp. 5, 7–8, 19, 28, 37, 46, 55, 60, 65–66, 68, 76–77, 79, 82, 85, 89, 91, 102, 109, 119, 150–152)

Karma – The law of cause and effect in action. It governs the life of the ego but becomes irrelevant once one realizes their true nature. (pp. 7, 46, 65–66, 70, 161)

Mind – The collection of thoughts, memories, and identities. It is not the Self but a tool that, when identified with, leads to suffering. (pp. 7, 16, 19, 22–24, 27, 40, 45–46, 52, 56–58, 69, 73, 77–78, 82, 84, 89, 97, 105, 115, 126, 159, 161)

Reality – That which is unchanging, eternal, formless, and without attributes. In Sri Ashish's framework, Reality is even prior to Consciousness. (pp. 7, 16–17, 19–25, 27, 29, 49, 58–59, 64, 69, 129, 159)

Remembrance – The process of re-recognizing our true nature as the Self. It is not new knowledge but the uncovering of what has always been. (pp. 36, 42)

Right Understanding – The first pillar of the Three-Fold Path. It involves seeing through illusions and recognizing the truth of non-separation. (pp. 7, 33, 37, 45, 47, 49, 51, 53, 55, 57, 59, 61, 63, 65, 67, 69)

Right Practice – The second pillar. Practical tools and approaches such as silence, surrender, meditation, and self-inquiry to stabilize awareness. (pp. 7, 33, 37, 69, 73, 75, 77, 79, 81, 83, 85, 87, 89, 91, 93, 95, 97, 99, 101, 164)

Right Experience – The third pillar. The direct realization and abiding in the Self beyond concepts or identities — the culmination of the Path. (pp. 8, 33, 37, 105, 107, 109, 111, 113, 115, 117, 119, 121, 123, 125, 127–129)

Samadhi – The state of absorption in the Self. A deep stillness beyond thought, emotion, or identity. (pp. 80)

Sat – Truth. Often used to refer to that which is changeless, eternal, and ever-present — the true nature of Self. (pp. 13, 21–22, 24, 28, 36, 146)

Self (with capital S) – The impersonal, infinite reality that is our true nature. Not the egoic self but the pure awareness or Being. (pp. 3, 7–8, 17, 20–21, 33, 37, 45, 58, 62, 64–65, 73, 78, 87, 101, 106, 108, 116, 122, 127, 129, 135, 138, 144, 151–152, 161, 163–164)

Self-Inquiry – The question "Who am I?" used as a method to trace the sense of "I" back to its source, revealing the Self. (pp. 7, 78, 101, 135, 138, 163–164)

Silence – Not merely the absence of sound, but the absence of mental noise and identification. Silence is seen as the language of Truth. (pp. 7, 16–17, 33, 39, 45–46, 52, 56–57, 69, 84, 86, 102, 105, 116, 137, 150, 163–164)

Stillness – A state where the mind has ceased its movements. In stillness, the Self is revealed. (pp. 7, 13, 16–17, 28, 33, 46, 54, 57, 69, 80–81, 84, 93, 97, 102, 106, 108, 112, 116, 151–152, 163–164)

Surrender – The letting go of control, ego, and resistance. Surrendering to what is allows the dissolution of false identity. (pp. 7, 39, 77, 97–98, 102, 164)

Transcendence – Going beyond identification with the body, mind, or even the sense of "I AM" to realize and abide as pure Reality. (pp. 8, 119)

Truth – Not conceptual truth, but the direct realization of what is — the Self, unconditioned and eternal. (pp. 7–8, 13, 16–17, 20, 33, 37, 39, 45, 47, 49–51, 53–57, 59, 61–65, 67, 69, 73, 75, 77–81, 83–85, 87, 89, 91, 93–95, 97, 99, 101–102, 105, 107, 109, 111–113, 115–117, 119, 121–123, 125, 127, 129, 144, 151–152)

Notes

www.ingramcontent.com/pod-product-compliance
Lightning Source LLC
Chambersburg PA
CBHW052003090426
42741CB00008B/1520